F *Corporations* *and* *Partnerships*

John C. Howell

AN EASY, DO-IT-YOURSELF GUIDE

LIBERTY HOUSE

FIRST EDITION

FOURTH PRINTING

Copyright © 1986 by John C. Howell

Printed in the United States of America

Published by:
  LIBERTY HOUSE
  A Division of
  TAB BOOKS Inc.
  Blue Ridge Summit, PA 17294

Library of Congress Cataloging in Publication
Data

Howell, John Cotton, 1926–
  Forming corporations and partnerships.

  Includes index.
  1. Corporation law—United States—Popular
works.
  2. Partnership—United States—Popular works.
  I. Title.
  KF1414.6.H673   1986b   346.73'066   86-27836
                          347.30666
  ISBN 0-8306-3143-7 (pbk.)

    TAB BOOKS Inc. offers software for
    sale. For information and a catalog,
  please contact TAB Software Department,
    Blue Ridge Summit, PA 17294-0850.

Questions regarding the content of this book
should be addressed to:

    Reader Inquiry Branch
    TAB BOOKS Inc.
    Blue Ridge Summit, PA 17294-0214

Cover photograph courtesy of Hampton National
Historic Site
Photographer Susan H. Cleveland

Contents

PART III SOLE PROPRIETORSHIP

Preface

The free enterprise system in America has sparked a conflagration of business activity throughout the world which will sketch a new chapter of human history. Small business owners, executives and entrepreneurs have seen more changes in our business community during the past 40 years than the preceding 200. As our nation emerges from the post-industrial revolution, it enters onto the stage of increased activity in the areas of electronics, computers, and communications, to name just a few. The advances in the business community have been a source of great pride for those involved in our free enterprise system.

The industrial revolution is now over and the American work place has been undergoing a radical change. Small business has become big business. More than 15 million small business firms, with that figure increasing at a rate of several hundred-thousands per year, generate a large part of our gross national product, provide employment for millions of people, and form a solid foundation for a grand economic system.

Most of the small businesses that are contributing to these advances are one of three types of business organizations: a corporation, a partnership (general or limited), or a sole proprietorship.

This book explains each of these types of business organizations and the benefits and disadvantages of each. Also included are descriptions of the necessary forms and complete step-by-step instructions. With or without an attorney, you can now form your own corporation, prepare your own partnership agreement or start a sole proprietorship easily, inexpensively and legally in every state.

Our remedies in ourselves do lie
Which we ascribe to Heaven.

— William Shakespeare.

How to Form Your Own Corporation

Part I
Selection of a
Business Entity

A corporation has been defined by the United States Supreme Court as "an artificial being, invisible, intangible, and existing only in contemplation of law." (Dartmouth College v. Woodward, 4 Wheat 518, 4 L ed 629). While the next two paragraphs provide more formal legal definitions, the balance of this chapter will explain the corporation in simpler terms.

The Supreme Court of Missouri has defined it as follows:

A corporation may be described as being an artificial being, existing only in contemplation of law; a legal entity, a fictitious person, vested by law with the capacity of taking and granting property and transacting business as an individual. It is composed of a number of individuals, authorized to act as if they were one person. The individual stockholders are the constituents or component parts through whose intelligence, judgment, and discretion the corporation acts. The affairs of a corporation cannot in many cases be conveniently conducted and managed by the stockholders, for they are often numerous and widely separated; yet they, in reality, compose the body corporate. (Jones v. Williams, et al, 139 Mo 1, 39 S.W. 486, 490 [1897])

One of the many definitions given in *Black's Law Dictionary* is that a corporation is:

An artificial person or legal entity created by or under the authority of the laws of a state or nation, composed, in some rare instances, of a single person and his successors, being the incumbents of a particular office, but ordinarily consisting of an association of numerous individuals. Such entity subsists as a body politic under a special denomination, which is regarded in law as having a personality and existence distinct from that of its several members, and which is, by the same authority, vested with the capacity of continuous succession, irrespective of changes in its membership, either in perpetuity or for a limited term of years, and of acting as a unit or single individual in matters relating to the scope of the powers and authorities conferred upon such bodies by law.

A simpler way to describe a corporation is that it is a separate legal entity which can be created by following the steps set out in the statutes of your state. While these legal definitions are generally approved as correct descriptions of a corporation, it is within the power of the legislature of your state to define a corporation. If an association falls within that definition, the courts will recognize the definition as legally binding. On the other hand, the federal government has a separate definition that is required for use in applying the tax code. The important thing for you to know is that a corporation is a distinct entity, separate from you, even though you may own substantially all of the stock and conduct most of the activities of the corporation.

Types of Corporations

Corporations fall into four broad classifications: public, private or profit-making, quasi-public, and nonprofit. In addition, they will be classified as foreign or domestic, depending on where the incorporation takes place.

A public corporation is one created for public purposes only. It is connected with the administration of the government. Examples are states, school districts, cities, and counties. Quasi-public is a term applied to corporations which are not strictly public in the sense of being organized for governmental purposes. Quasi-public corporations are those which operate by contributing to the comfort, convenience, and welfare of the general public. Examples are gas, water, electric, and other utility companies. Private corporations are created for private purposes as distinguished from those purely public and are generally thought of as business entities carrying on activities for profit-making purposes. A profit-making corporation is primarily a business corporation organized with a view toward gains that are to be distributed among its members. A nonprofit corporation, sometimes referred to as eleemosynary, is one created for or devoted to charitable purposes or those supported by charity. Foreign corporations are those organized in another state or country. A domestic corporation is one organized within the state. It is not generally recommended that you organize your corporation in a foreign state or jurisdiction.

Basically, the character of a corporation is determined by the object of its formation and the nature of its business. The character of a corporation may not be changed by calling it something different from that specified in its articles of incorporation. Because of this requirement, you should make certain that the articles sufficiently describe and define the purposes for which the corporation is established.

Alternative Business Entities Available

When you are considering whether to form a corporation, you should know what options are available and how their characteristics compare to those of corporations. Some of the most important items to consider in making a decision include:
- liability exposure,
- tax costs and tax considerations,
- centralization of management,
- advantages of raising capital through issuance of stock,
- ability to attract and keep key personnel through various fringe benefits or participation as stockholders,
- the practical convenience of the various forms in which a business might be conducted.

As the risk of potential personal liability increases, whether from the nature of the business or from the extent of your assets, the value of eliminating personal liability increases and so does the advantage of the corporate form. The small expenses involved in setting up a corporation are relatively insignificant when compared with the liability factors.

Other Business Entities

The three forms of business organization most commonly used are corporation, partnership, and sole proprietorship. The partnership and sole proprietorship are discussed in detail in Parts II and III of this book.

Factors to Consider in Selection of A Business Entity

No matter what form of business entity you ultimately decide to use, it is important to know what controlling factors to consider. The major items are listed and discussed below.

Simplicity

The sole proprietorship is the least complicated. You can start a partnership with a handshake or with a lengthy written partnership agreement, depending on the nature of the business and the persons involved. Any partner can dissolve a partnership at will in the absence of a contract to the contrary. This allows one partner to freely terminate a partnership without the consent of the other partners. The death of one of the partners automatically ends the partnership. The trend in the business community is to incorporate. Recent changes in state corporation statutes make incorporation simple and economical.

Organizational Flexibility

The corporate form permits great variation in operation and development. For example, greater or lesser powers may be bestowed on a governing board of directors by a larger or smaller number of members. That is, smaller working committees with specified powers may be established for purposes such as overall management on a temporary basis. Other examples include an executive committee to operate in special fields on a continuing basis, a finance committee, or a retirement committee. Departments may be created, branches established, and offices created at various levels with supervisory personnel below them in any number of levels required by the business. The modern corporate form has developed an almost unlimited flexibility of managerial organization.

Financing

In the early stages of a business enterprise, financing will probably depend on the personal credit of the principals. However, this is generally true in any form of business. When the business accumulates assets and shows earning power, it will establish its own credit without involving the principals. The availability of corporate stock will be important in providing additional capacity to attract financing either through private or public offering of stock.

Continuity

Continuity is assured through the corporate form better than through any other. A partnership terminates upon the death of a partner and a final accounting becomes necessary. This can be a burden during inconvenient times. A corporation continues to exist no matter how many of its directors, officers or stockholders die. Title to property, contracts, and other rights remain unaffected, and the business can continue to operate. Stock transfers can be accomplished speedily and new elections can be held as often as needed. The corporation is a vehicle ideally suited for continuing a business beyond a single generation, and its advantage grows in importance with the growth of the business.

Transferability of Shares

As a business prospers, there are certain occasions in which
the owners may wish to distribute all or part of the ownership to others. This is not feasible in a sole proprietorship, but
is easy and convenient through the corporate form by transfers
of stock.

Good Will

If good will is likely to develop into an asset of substantial
value, it is advantageous for the corporate form to accumulate
good will and maintain public identification.

Compensation Arrangements

The corporate form makes it possible to attract and reward
talent with stock options, stock purchases, deferred compensation arrangements, participation of the owners in pension
and profit sharing plans, group insurance benefits, and other
benefits.

Estate Liquidity

The possible future sale of corporate shares and the possible
creation of a public market hold the promise of easing estate
liquidity problems. Even when this is not likely to occur, the
corporate form may make the way easier to accumulate earnings and pay for insurance to facilitate the redemption of
shares owned by a deceased stockholder.

Splitting Income Among the Family

A family partnership is a suitable method for splitting income and capital values among children and other members
of the family, but the corporate form has this same flexibility. The corporation is also well-suited for capital appreciation.

Summary of Corporate Advantages

In summary it may be said that incorporation is advantageous because of the following ten reasons:

- The owners, stockholders, or principals have no individual liability other than the capital contribution in stock payments.
- Corporations are perpetual.
- The corporation is a separate entity from the stockholders.
- Corporations can sue and be sued, and hold and deal in property.
- Stock can ordinarily be sold or otherwise transferred at will.
- Corporations can raise capital by the issuance of new stock, bonds, or other securities.
- A board of directors is the center of authority, acting by majority agreement.
- As a separate entity, a corporation has credit possibilities apart from stockholders, and stock is sometimes available as collateral.
- Incorporation is very popular in the business community.
- Tax advantages and fringe benefits for owners.

Where to Incorporate:
Avoiding the "Foreign Corporation Trap"

Many years ago it was considered advantageous to incorporate in some state other than your own where there were more liberal laws. This was called "corporate forum shopping." This practice is no longer advisable and has more disadvantages than advantages. Now it is almost universally accepted that the state of principal business activity is the state favored for incorporation. In the case of local business operations, it is especially important to incorporate in your state. Virtually all states have simplified incorporation statutes, most of which are patterned after the Model Business Corporation Act of the Committee on Corporate Laws of the American Bar Association.

Considering current circumstances, incorporation in another state will usually add to organizational and recurring operational costs, including tax costs, and the extra, and unnecessary, costs for your "foreign agent." A further disadvantage may be the possibility of a suit against the corporation in what will likely be an inconvenient and hostile foreign forum. Moreover, your company will be considered a foreign corporation in the courts of your home state. This could subject you to attachment proceedings (seizure of property by legal authority) and other procedural disadvantages. Also, if you incorporate in another state, you will be required to register in your state as a foreign corporation before you can legitimately carry on a local business in your state. Usually, the expenses to register a foreign corporation to do business in your state are much greater than the cost of forming a corporation there. Moreover, you will be required to pay a "resident agent" fee to a resident agent in the foreign state. It is, of course, understandable that these "foreign agents" recommend others to incorporate in their state. It follows that the outdated advice to go forum shopping to incorporate could be a costly mistake. For example, in some states the filing fee to register a foreign corporation to do business within the state is much more than the fees to form a domestic corporation.

During the past 30 years we have seen much greater uniformity in the corporate laws of all states. However, if you still wish to go shopping for a foreign corporate forum, it is to your advantage to acquire good legal advice before making a final decision.

Steps in Creating and Organizing Your Corporation

Establishing your corporation is usually a simple matter once you determine the state's requirements. The procedure is set out in each state statute. Most statutes, based on the Model Act, require nothing more than these simple steps:

- Selection of the name.
- Filling out a form of articles of incorporation; in some states these are furnished by the secretary of state.
- Filing the form along with the filing fees.
- Getting a corporate kit.
- Holding an organizational meeting.
- Preparing minutes of the organizational meeting.

The secretary of state usually has necessary forms, and frequently has information booklets summarizing the statutes. You can purchase a corporate kit or you can make one.

A copy of your state corporation statutes may be obtained in any law library. A summary of each of the state statutes is contained in the Martindale-Hubbell Law Directory found in most law libraries. Either write, call, or visit the state office which administers the corporation laws to obtain forms and information on filing fees. Your letter can be based on this sample:

Dear Sir or Madam:
   I wish to form a new corporation in this state and request
that you send me the forms and information necessary
to form a private profit-making corporation in this state.
Please forward me a schedule of all fees required for
incorporation.

Almost invariably each state office has several people whose
primary responsibilities and duties are to assist in filing these
papers and to keep the corporate records of the state. Usually they are helpful and cooperative in giving any information
or assistance needed. The following list contains all the steps
necessary to complete your incorporation. Note that some of
these steps are not required in all states.

   • Determine the Availability of Your Corporate Name. You
certainly would not name your corporation General Motors,
Inc., AT&T, or IBM because these are among the many names
already taken. Simply call or write to the secretary of state
to see if the name you want to use is available. Most states
will give this information on the telephone, but won't
guarantee the availability of the name; other states require
a letter. If you wish, a name can be reserved by paying a
nominal fee, but this is usually a waste of time, money, and
effort unless you expect to have some extensive delay in filing. Once you learn that the desired name is available, you
simply fill out the papers and file them. The forms following
this section, which include the essential papers, can be used
in getting your new corporation organized.
   • File the Articles of Incorporation. Most states have forms
for completion of these articles. Form 1 is taken from the Model
Act and is representative of most states. You simply follow
the requirements of your state statutes.
   Completion of the form is a relatively simple matter, but
there are several items you should consider. These suggestions include the practice of most people who form their own
corporations. The duration is usually filled in as "perpetual."
Describe the basic purpose as suggested by the descriptions
in Appendix A and add the phrase "and all other acts authorized by law." In some states the filing fee is determined by

the aggregate number of shares the corporation is authorized to issue. In these states you should authorize the minimum number on the sliding scale to keep the filing fee as low as possible.

It is important to distinguish authorized shares (those you may or may not wish to issue) from issued shares (those actually issued by the corporation). In a small corporation you may wish to issue only a few shares in the beginning — perhaps no more than 100 to 500 shares among 10,000 to 50,000 authorized shares. The idea is to have additional authorized shares that can be issued later when other capital is needed in the corporation. You should indicate cumulative voting of shares of stock as authorized, and that there shall be no provisions limiting or denying to shareholders the pre-emptive right to acquire additional or treasury shares of the corporation. The name of the initial registered agent should be the principal person responsible for the creation and operation of the business.

• Pay Filing Fees. These vary on the average from $10 to about $40. A few states are somewhat higher. Determine from the secretary of state or from the statutes whether payment of any other fees or taxes are required and whether any other notice, publication, or filings are required in your state.

• Hold Organizational Meetings. Legally, and technically, the certificate of the secretary of state or other approval of the initial corporate papers is considered to be the creation of a corporation. It has a legal existence by virtue of the completion of the statutory requirements and the declaration of the state official that the corporation is in existence. However, in a practical sense, it is necessary to take formal steps to make the corporation an operating entity. This procedure includes the election of officers and directors, the subscription and payment of capital stock, adoption of bylaws, and other steps necessary to provide the legal entity with the capacity to actually transact business. This is accomplished by the holding of formal organizational meetings. In some states these meetings are held by the incorporators, and in others by the stockholders or the members of the board of directors listed or designated in the articles of incorporation.

The specific procedural steps usually taken at these meetings include: the election of directors; adoption of bylaws; designation of principal corporate office and any branch offices; adoption of the corporate seal and stock certificates; authorizing the issuance of stock; accepting payment of the required amount for commencement of business; designation of official corporate record books; adoption of a plan under Section 1244 of the Internal Revenue Code; approval of the filing of the Articles of Incorporation; and any other appropriate procedural requirements. In some circumstances additional items may be covered at these meetings.

In a small corporation where the incorporators, stockholders, members of the board of directors, and the officers consist of a small group of people, the organizational meeting of the board of directors is usually a formality where the procedures and steps taken at the first meeting of incorporators are approved and the board takes any other action that may be needed. The board of directors should formally approve action taken at any other organizational meetings, and have this approval noted in the minutes of the meeting. The statutes, articles of incorporation, and bylaws should be reviewed to ensure that the board of directors approves all required items.

Generally, the secretary is the person who keeps the corporate books and has the responsibility of preparing proper and appropriate records of the organizational and other meetings. In the event you do not have a corporate kit or you decide to prepare your own, the forms in this book can be adopted as they are, or you can revise them to fit your situation.

• Local Filings. A few states have a provision for filing with local authorities, usually the county or city clerk. This is normally a notice of incorporation to be placed on record by the clerk. When you file with the secretary of state you should ask whether any other formalities are required in your state. This rule of local filings is a holdover from the older statutory enactments and is no longer found in the modern statutes.

• Prepare and Approve Bylaws. The bylaws are extremely important in the sense that they are the governing rules for the internal operations of the corporation. However, it is a general practice in a small corporation to grant extensive powers and authority to the officers and directors for carrying on the business operations of the corporation. This makes it unnecessary to have frequent or regular formal meetings of the board of directors or stockholders. Most corporate kits have a suggested form for bylaws providing for full and complete powers and authority in the officers and directors.

• Obtain Corporate Kit. Most kits contain a corporate seal, stock register, stock certificate book, bylaws, and minutes book. These can be purchased at most large stationery stores or you can prepare one yourself. Two companies that regularly advertise corporate kits for lawyers in legal publications are:

Excelsior-Legal New York:	(Order from the branch nearest you) 62 White Street New York, NY 10013
Georgia:	P.O. Box 889 Norcross, GA 30091
Illinois:	P.O. Box 4956 Chicago, IL 60680
Texas:	P.O. Box 5683 Arlington, TX 76011

CORPEX
    Dept. A
    480 Canal Street
    New York, NY 10013

Prices of these kits range from $35.00 to $50.00 each.

Following are 18 commonly used forms for establishing and maintaining a corporation.

FORM 1: Articles of Incorporation

We, the undersigned, natural persons of the age of _____ years or more, acting as incorporators of a corporation under the laws of the state of _____, adopt the following articles of incorporation for such corporation:

First: The name of the corporation is_____.

Second: The period of its duration is _____.

Third: The purpose or purposes for which the corporation is organized are _____.

Fourth: The aggregate number of shares which the corporation shall have authority to issue is _____.

Fifth: The corporation will not commence business until at least _____ Dollars have been received by it as consideration for the issuance of shares.

Sixth: Cumulative voting of shares of stock [is], [is not] authorized.

Seventh: Provisions limiting or denying to shareholders the pre-emptive right to acquire additional or treasury shares of the corporation are: _____.

Eighth: Provisions for the regulation of the internal affairs of the corporation are: _____.

Ninth: The address of the initial registered office of the corporation is _____, and the name of its initial registered at such address is _____.

Tenth: Address of the principal place of business _____
_____ .

Eleventh: The number of directors constituting the initial board of directors of the corporation is ___, and the names and addresses of the persons who are to serve as directors until the first annual meeting of shareholders or until their successors are elected and shall qualify are:

Name   Address

_____   _____
_____   _____
_____   _____

Twelfth: The name and address of each incorporator is:

Name   Address

_____   _____
_____   _____
_____   _____

(Date)   _____
                              _____
                              _____

                                      Incorporators
(Verification)

FORM 2: Waiver of Notice of the Organization Meeting

We, the undersigned, being all the incorporators [and/or the members of the board of directors] named in the Articles of Incorporation of the above corporation [and/or the stockholders], hereby agree and consent that the organization meeting thereof be held on the date and the time and place stated below and hereby waive all notice of such meeting and of any adjournment thereof.

Place of Meeting: _____
Date of Meeting: _____
Time of Meeting: _____
(Date)   _____

                                      (Signatures)
                              _____
                              _____

FORM 3: Minutes of the Organizational Meeting

The organizational meeting of the incorporators [and/or the stockholders and/or the members of the board of directors] of _____was held at_____on_____at_____
The following were present: _____
_____

being all the incorporators [and/or the stockholders and/or the members of the board of directors] of the corporation.
_____ was appointed chairman of the meeting and_____was appointed secretary.
The secretary then presented and read to the meeting the waiver of notice of the meeting, subscribed by all the persons named in the Articles of Incorporation, and it was ordered that it be appended to the minutes of the meeting.
The secretary then presented and read to the meeting a copy of the Articles of Incorporation and reported that on ____ the original thereof was filed in the office of the Secretary of State of this state. The copy of the Articles of Incorporation was ordered appended to the minutes of the meeting.
The chairman then stated that nominations were in order for election of directors of the corporation to hold office until the first annual meeting of stockholders and until their successors shall be elected and shall qualify.
The following persons were nominated: _____
_____
_____

No further nominations being made, nominations were closed and a vote was taken. After the vote had been counted, the chairman declared that the foregoing named nominees were elected directors of the corporation.
The secretary then presented to the meeting a proposed form of bylaws which were read to the meeting, considered, and upon motion duly made, seconded and carried, were adopted as and for the bylaws of the corporation and ordered appended to the minutes of the meeting.

Upon motion duly made, seconded, and unanimously carried, it was Further Resolved, that the specimen stock certificate presented to the meeting be and hereby is adopted as the form of certificate of stock to be issued to represent shares in the corporation;

Further Resolved, that the corporate record book, including the stock transfer ledger, be and hereby is adopted as the record book, stock transfer book, and ledger of the corporation;

Further Resolved, that the board of directors be and hereby is authorized to issue the unsubscribed capital stock of the corporation at such time and in such amounts as it shall determine, and to accept the payment thereof, in cash or services or such other property as the board may deem necessary for the business of the corporation;

Further Resolved, that the corporate seal presented to the meeting by the secretary be and the same is hereby adopted as the seal of the corporation;

Further Resolved, that the corporation be and hereby is authorized and directed to accept the payment of capital required for the commencement of business, and that the same be properly reflected upon the books and records of the corporation;

Further Resolved, that the principal office of the corporation be and hereby is designated as _____ and the board of directors is hereby authorized to change said designation as it deems proper and it may designate branch offices from time to time as it shall, in its judgment, determine to be necessary and proper;

Further Resolved, that a plan for the issuance of common stock of the corporation to qualify under the provisions of Section 1244 of the Internal Revenue Code, which plan was read to the meeting, be and the same is hereby adopted, approved, and confirmed by the corporation, and the officers and directors of the corporation are hereby authorized and directed to take all steps, procedures, and action necessary to implement the plan;

Further Resolved, that all other actions, notifications, publications, filings, and any other procedural requirements for the full authorization of this corporation to commence the business for which it was created be completed by the

secretary, and that a record thereof be filed in the corporate
records of the corporation.

Upon motion duly made, seconded, and carried, it was

Resolved, that the signing of these minutes shall constitute
full ratification thereof and waiver of notice of the meeting
by the signatories.

There being no further business before the meeting, on motion duly made, seconded, and carried, the meeting adjourned.

(Date)   _____
                                      Chairman

                         _____
                                      Secretary

FORM 4: Call and Waiver of Notice
of Organizational Meeting

We, the undersigned, being all of the directors [and/or the
incorporators and/or the stockholders] of _____,
hereby call the organizational meeting of the corporation, to
consider and transact any business whatsoever that may be
brought before the meeting, and we hereby fix _____
at_____as the place of the meeting, and hereby
waive any and all requirements by statute, bylaws, or otherwise, as to notice of the time, place, and purposes of the
meeting, and consent that the meeting be held at the time and
place set out above and to the transaction thereat or at any
adjournment thereof of any business whatsoever that may be
brought before the meeting, including, without any limitation
on the scope of the foregoing, the adoption of bylaws, election
of officers, and authorization of issuance of stock.

(Date)   (Signatures)

FORM 5: Minutes of the First Meeting of the Board of Directors

Pursuant to _____, the Board of Directors of _____, elected at the organizational meeting of the incorporation on _____, assembled and held its first meeting at [place] on [date] at [time].

Present at the meeting were _____, _____, and _____, being all of the directors. _____ called the meeting to order, and on motion duly made and seconded, he was appointed temporary chairman, and _____ was appointed temporary secretary.

The election of officers was thereupon declared to be in order. The following were named and duly elected: _____, president;_____, vice-president; and_____, as secretary-treasurer. _____ took the chair and presided at the meeting.

The secretary presented a form of bylaws (adopted by the incorporators and/or the stockholders) for the regulation of the affairs of the corporation, which were read section by section.

On motion duly made, seconded, and carried, it was

Resolved, that the bylaws submitted at and read to this meeting be, and the same hereby are, approved as and for the bylaws of this corporation, and that the secretary be, and she hereby is, instructed to certify the bylaws and cause the same to be inserted in the minutes book of this corporation, and to certify a copy of the bylaws, which shall be kept at the principal office of this corporation and open to inspection by stockholders at all reasonable times during office hours.

On motion duly made, seconded and carried, it was

Resolved, that the seal (adopted by the incorporation and/or stockholders), an impression of which is herewith affixed, be adopted as the corporate seal of the corporation.

[corporate seal]

The secretary was authorized and directed to procure the proper corporate books.

On motion duly made, seconded, and carried, it was

Resolved, that [name of bank] of the City of _____,
State of _____, be, and it is, hereby selected as a
depositary for the money, funds, and credits of this corporation and that_____and_____be, and they are
authorized and empowered to draw checks on the above
depositary, against the account for this corporation with the
depositary, and to endorse in the name of this corporation and
receive payment of all checks, drafts, and commercial papers
payable to this corporation either as payee or endorsee;

Further Resolved, that the certification of the secretary of
this corporation as to the election and appointment of persons
so authorized to sign such checks and as to the signatures of
such persons shall be binding on this corporation;

Further Resolved, that the secretary of this corporation be,
and she hereby is, authorized and directed to deliver to said
bank a copy of these resolutions properly certified by her.

On motion duly made, seconded, and carried, it was

Resolved, that the principal office of the corporation for the
transaction of its business be, and it hereby is, fixed at __
_____.

Further Resolved, that the specimen stock certificate
presented to this meeting be and hereby is approved as the
form of certificate of stock to be issued to represent shares
in the corporation;

Further Resolved, that the corporate record book, including
the stock transfer ledger, be and hereby is approved as the
record book and stock transfer ledger of the corporation;

Further Resolved, that the treasurer of the corporation be
and hereby is authorized to pay all charges and expenses in-
cident to or arising out of the organization of the corporation
and to reimburse any person who has made any disbursement
therefor;

Further Resolved, that all actions taken at the organizational
meeting of the incorporators, and/or the stockholders, and/or
the members of the board of directors designated in the Articles of Incorporation, as reflected by the minutes of said
meeting, be and they are hereby ratified, confirmed, and
approved;

Further Resolved, that the officers of this corporation take such other procedural action as may be necessary for this corporation to commence the transaction of business in this state.

There being no further business, the meeting was adjourned.

_____
Secretary

FORM 6: Bylaws

Article 1: Offices

The principal office of the corporation shall be located at _____. The board of directors shall have the power and authority to establish and maintain branch or subordinate offices at any other location either within this state or in any other state or country.

Article 2: Stockholders

Section 1. Annual Meetings: The annual meeting of the stockholders shall be held on the_____day of the month of _____ in each year, beginning with the year 19____, at the hour of_____o'clock, for the purpose of electing directors and for the transaction of such other business as may come before the meeting. If the day fixed for the annual meeting shall be a legal holiday in the state of incorporation, such meeting shall be held on the next succeeding business day. If the election of directors is not held on the day designated herein for any annual meeting of the shareholders, or at any adjournment thereof, the board of directors shall cause the election to be held at a special meeting of the stockholders as soon thereafter as is convenient.

Section 2. Special Meetings: Special meetings of the stockholders, for any purpose or purposes, unless otherwise prescribed by statute, may be called by the president or by the board of directors, and shall be called by the president at the request of the holders of not less than_____percent of all the outstanding shares of the corporation entitled to vote at the meeting.

Section 3: Place of Meeting: The board of directors may designate any place within the state of incorporation or within any other state as the place of meeting for any annual meeting or for any special meeting called by the board of directors. A waiver of notice signed by all stockholders entitled to vote at a meeting may designate any place, either within the state of incorporation or in any other state, as the place for the holding of such meeting. If no designation is made, or if a special meeting is otherwise called, the place of the meeting shall be the principal office of the corporation as designated pursuant to Article 1.

Section 4. Notice of Meeting: Written or printed notice stating the place, day, and hour of the meeting and, in case of a special meeting, the purpose or purposes for which the meeting is called, shall be delivered not less than _____ nor more than _____ days before the date of the meeting, either personally or by mail, by or at the direction of the president, or the secretary, or the officer or persons calling the meeting, to each shareholder of record entitled to vote at such meeting. If mailed, such notice shall be deemed to be delivered when deposited in the United States mail, addressed to the shareholder at his address as it appears on the stock transfer books of the corporation with postage thereon prepaid. Notice of each meeting shall also be mailed to holders of stock not entitled to vote, if any, as herein provided, but lack of such notice shall not affect the legality of any meeting otherwise properly called and noticed.

Section 5. Closing of Stock Transfer Books: For the purpose of determining stockholders entitled to notice of, or to vote at, any meeting of stockholders or any adjournment thereof, or stockholders entitled to receive payment of any dividend, or to make a determination of shareholders for any other purpose, the board of directors of the corporation may provide that the stock transfer books shall be closed for a stated period, but not to exceed_____days. If the stock transfer books shall be closed for the purpose of determining stockholders entitled to notice of, or to vote at, a meeting of stockholders, such books shall be closed for at least ____ days preceding such meeting. In lieu of closing the stock transfer books, the board of directors may fix in advance a date as the record date for any such determination of stockholders, such date in any event to be not more than _____ days, and in case of a meeting of stockholders, not less than _____ days, prior to the date on which the particular action requiring such determination of stockholders is to be taken.

If the stock transfer books are not closed and no record date is fixed for the determination of stockholders entitled to notice of, or to vote at, a meeting of stockholders, or of stockholders entitled to receive payment of a dividend, the date that notice of the meeting is mailed or the date on which the resolution of the board of directors declaring such dividend is adopted, as the case may be, shall be the record date for such determination of stockholders. When a determination of stockholders entitled to vote at any meeting of stockholders has been made as provided in this section, such determination shall apply to any adjournment thereof except where the determination has been made through the closing of the stock transfer books and the stated period of closing has expired.

Section 6. Quorum Requirements for Stockholder Meetings. A majority of the outstanding shares of the corporation entitled to vote, represented in person or by proxy, shall constitute a quorum at a meeting of stockholders. If less than a majority of such outstanding shares are represented at a meeting, a majority of the shares so represented may adjourn the meeting from time to time without notice. At such adjourned meeting at which a quorum is present or represented, any business may be transacted that might have been transacted at the meeting as originally notified. The stockholders present at a duly organized meeting may continue to transact business until adjournment, notwithstanding the withdrawal of enough stockholders to leave less than a quorum.

Section 7. Voting of Shares: Subject to the provisions of any applicable law, the Articles of Incorporation or these bylaws concerning cumulative voting, each outstanding share entitled to vote shall be entitled to one vote on each matter submitted to a vote at a meeting of stockholders.

Section 8. Proxies: At all meetings of stockholders, a stockholder may vote by proxy executed in writing by the stockholder or by his duly authorized attorney in fact. Such proxy shall be filed with the secretary of the corporation before or at the time of the meeting. No proxy shall be valid after _____ months from the date of its execution unless otherwise provided in the proxy.

Article 3: Board of Directors

Section 1. Powers and Duties: The business and affairs of the corporation shall be managed by its board of directors.

Section 2. Qualifications of Members: The number of directors of the corporation shall be _____. Directors shall be elected at the annual meeting of stockholders, and the term of office of each director shall be until the next annual meeting of stockholders and the election and qualification of his successor. Directors need not be residents of the state of incorporation, but shall be stockholders of the corporation.

Section 3. Regular Meetings: A regular meeting of the board of directors shall be held without notice other than this bylaw immediately after, and at the same place as, the annual meeting of stockholders. The board of directors may provide, by resolution, the time and place for holding additional regular meetings without other notice than such resolution. Additional regular meetings shall be held at the principal office of the corporation in the absence of any designation in the resolution.

Section 4. Special Meetings: Special meetings of the board of directors may be called by, or at the request of, the president or any two directors, and shall be held at the principal office of the corporation or at such other place as the directors may determine.

Section 5. Notice: Notice of any special meeting shall be given at least _____ hours before the time fixed for the meeting, by written notice delivered personally or mailed to each director at his business address or by telegram. If mailed, such notice shall be deemed to be delivered when deposited in the United States mail so addressed, with postage thereon prepaid, not less than___days prior to the commencement of the above stated notice period. If notice is given by telegram, such notice shall be deemed to be delivered when the telegram is delivered to the telegraph company. Any director may waive notice of any meeting. The attendance of a director at a meeting shall constitute a waiver of notice of such meeting, except where a director attends a meeting for the express purpose of objecting to the transaction of any business because the meeting is not lawfully called or convened. Neither the business to be transacted at, nor the purpose of, any regular or special meeting of the board of directors need be specified in the notice or waiver of notice of such meeting.

Section 6. Quorum: A majority of the number of directors fixed by these bylaws shall constitute a quorum for the transaction of business at any meeting of the board of directors, but if less than such majority is present at a meeting, a majority of the directors present may adjourn the meeting from time to time without further notice.

Section 7. Board of Director Decisions: The act of the majority of the directors present at a meeting at which a quorum is present shall be the act of the board of directors.

Section 8. Compensation: By resolution of the board of directors, the directors may be paid their expenses, if any, of attendance of each meeting of the board of directors, and may be paid a fixed sum for attendance at each meeting of the board of directors or a stated salary as director. No such payment shall preclude any director from serving the corporation in any other capacity and receiving compensation therefor.

Article 4: Officers

Section 1. Number and Vacancies: The officers of the corporation shall be a president, one or more vice-presidents, a secretary, and a treasurer, each of whom shall be elected by the board of directors. Such other officers and assistant officers as may be deemed necessary may be elected or appointed by the board of directors. Any two or more offices may be held by the same person, except the office of president. A vacancy in any office because of death, resignation, removal, disqualification, or otherwise, may be filled by the board of directors for the unexpired portion of the term.

Section 2. Election, Term of Office, and Removal: The officers of the corporation to be elected by the board of directors shall be elected annually at the first meeting of the board of directors held after each annual meeting of the stockholders. If the election of officers is not held at such meeting, such election shall be held as soon thereafter as is convenient. Each officer shall hold office until his successor has been duly elected and qualifies, or until his death, or until he resigns or is removed in the manner hereinafter provided. Any officer or agent elected or appointed by the board of directors may be removed by the board of directors whenever in its judgment the best interests of the corporation would be served thereby, but such removal shall be without prejudice to the contract rights, if any, of the person so removed.

Section 3. Salaries: The salaries of the officers shall be fixed from time to time by the board of directors, and no officer shall be prevented from receiving such salary by reason of the fact that he is also a director of the corporation.

Section 4. Powers and Duties: The powers and duties of the several officers shall be as provided from time to time by resolution or other directive of the board of directors. In the absence of such provisions, the respective officers shall have the powers and shall discharge the duties customarily and usually held and performed by like officers of corporations similar in organization and business purposes to this corporation.

Article 5: Conduct of Business

Section 1. Contracts: The board of directors may authorize any officer or officers, agent or agents, to enter into any contract or execute and deliver any instrument in the name of, and on behalf of, the corporation, and such authority may be general or confined to specific instances.

Section 2. Loans: No loans shall be contracted on behalf of the corporation and no evidence of indebtedness shall be issued in its name unless authorized by a resolution of the board of directors. Such authority may be general or confined to specific instances.

Section 3. Checks, Drafts, or Orders: All checks, drafts, or other orders for the payment of money, notes, or other evidences of indebtedness issued in the name of the corporation shall be signed by such officer or officers, agent or agents, of the corporation and in such manner as shall from time to time be determined by resolution of the board of directors.

Section 4. Deposits: All funds of the corporation not otherwise employed shall be deposited from time to time to the credit of the corporation in such banks, trust companies, or other depositaries as the board of directors may select.

Article 6: Corporate Stock and Stock Transfers

Section 1. Certificates for Shares of Stock: Certificates representing shares of the corporation shall be in such form as shall be determined by the board of directors. Such certificates shall be signed by the president, or a vice-president, and by the secretary or an assistant secretary. All certificates for shares shall be consecutively numbered or otherwise identified. The name and address of the person to whom the shares represented thereby are issued, with the number of shares and date of issue, shall be entered on the stock transfer books of the corporation. All certificates surrendered to the corporation for transfer shall be canceled and no new certificate shall be issued until the former certificate for the like number of shares shall have been surrendered or canceled, except that in case of a lost, destroyed, or mutilated certificate a new one may be issued therefor on such terms and indemnity to the corporation as the board of directors may prescribe.

Section 2. Transfer of Shares of Stock on Books of Record: The transfer of shares of stock of the corporation shall be made in the manner required by law, and pursuant to procedures established by the board of directors. The corporation shall maintain stock transfer books, and any transfer shall be registered thereon only on request and surrender of the stock certificate representing the transferred shares, duly endorsed. The corporation shall have the absolute right to recognize as the owner of any shares of stock issued by it, the person or persons in whose name the certificate representing such shares stands according to the books of the corporation for all prop-

er corporate purposes, including the voting of the shares
represented by the certificate at a regular or special meeting
of stockholders, and the issuance and payment of dividends
on such shares.

Article 7: Fiscal Year

The fiscal year of the corporation shall be _____.

Article 8: Dividends

The board of directors may from time to time declare, and
the corporation may pay, dividends on its outstanding shares
in the manner and on the terms and conditions provided by
law and its Articles of Incorporation.

Article 9: Seal

The board of directors shall provide a corporate seal, which
shall be circular in form and shall have inscribed thereon the
name of the corporation and the state of incorporation and the
words "Corporate Seal." The seal shall be stamped or affixed
to such documents as may be prescribed by law or custom or
by the board of directors.

Article 10: Waiver of Notice

Whenever any notice is required to be given to any stockholder or director of the corporation under the provisions of
these bylaws or under the provisions of the Articles of Incorporation or under the provisions of law, a waiver thereof in
writing, signed by the person or persons entitled to such notice,
whether before or after the time stated therein, shall be
deemed equivalent to the giving of such notice.

Article 11: Amendments to These Bylaws

These bylaws may be altered, amended, or repealed and new
bylaws may be adopted by the board of directors at any regular
or special meeting of the board provided, however, that the

number of directors shall not be increased or decreased, nor shall the provisions of Article Two, concerning the stockholders, be substantially altered without the prior approval of the stockholders at a regular or special meeting of the stockholders, or by written consent. Changes in, and additions to, the bylaws by the board of directors shall be reported to the stockholders at their next regular meeting and shall be subject to the approval or disapproval of the stockholders at such meeting. If no action is then taken by the stockholders on a change in, or addition to, the bylaws, such change or addition shall be deemed to be fully approved and ratified by the stockholders.

FORM 7: Notice of Regular Meeting of the Board of Directors

Notice is hereby given that the regular [annual] meeting of the board of directors of _____ is hereby called to be held at [place] on [date] at [time], which meeting shall be for the purpose of_____.
(Date)   _____
                                                 Secretary

FORM 8: Waiver of Notice of Regular Meeting of the Board of Directors

The undersigned members of the board of directors of__ _____ waive notice of the next regular meeting of the board and consent and agree that a meeting of the board of directors may be held at the office of the company, [address], at [time], on [date], for the purpose of transacting all business properly presented to the meeting.

(Date)   (Signatures)

FORM 9: Notice of Special Meeting of the Board of Directors

Please take notice that a special meeting of the board of directors of _____ will be held at the office of the company at [time] on [date] at [address], for the purpose of _____.

(Date)

                                     _____
                                       Secretary

FORM 10: Waiver of Notice of Special Meeting of the Board of Directors

We, the undersigned, being all of the directors of_____, a corporation organized and existing under the laws of the State of _____, desiring to hold a special meeting of the directors of the corporation, hereby severally waive notice and publication of notice of such meeting, and we hereby severally consent and agree to the holding of such meeting of the directors of the corporation at [time] on [date] at [address], for the consideration and transaction of a proposition to _____ and for the transaction of any other business that may be legally done or brought up at the meeting, and we hereby further severally agree that any proceedings and any and all business transacted at this meeting and at any meeting or meetings to which the meeting may be adjourned, shall be as valid and legal, and as of the same force and effect, as if the meeting were held after due notice was given and published.

(Date)　　　　　　　　　　　　　　　　　　　　(Signatures)

FORM 11: Notice of Adjourned Meeting of the Board of Directors

To: _____, Director

You are hereby notified that the meeting of the board of directors of_____held at [time] on [date] at [address] was adjourned until [time] at [date] at the same location.

(Date)

                                        _____
                                        Secretary

FORM 12: Minutes of Special Meeting of the Board of Directors

The board of directors met pursuant to_____in special meeting in the office of the corporation, _____.

The meeting was called to order by the president, _____, and directors _____ and _____, consisting of all of the members of the board of directors, and all being present, the board commenced business.

The secretary then presented the _____ pursuant to which the meeting was held. There being no objections, it was ordered to be entered into the minutes.

The president then presented to the board the subject about which the meeting was called, to wit: _____.

The following action was taken: _____

There being no further business, the meeting was adjourned.

(Date)

                                        _____
                                        Secretary

FORM 13: Notice of Regular [or Special] Meeting of Stockholders

Notice is hereby given that _____ meeting of the stockholders of _____, a corporation organized and existing under the laws of the State of_____, will be held at the office of the corporation, at [time] on [date] at [address], for the purpose of _____.

(Date)   _____
                                                          Secretary

FORM 14: Notice of Annual Meeting of Stockholders

Notice is hereby given that the annual meeting of the stockholders of_____will be held at the office of the corporation, _____, on [date] at [time].
    Business to be transacted shall include the following items:
1. To elect directors for the ensuing year.
2. To receive and consider the financial statements and the reports of the affairs of the corporation for the year 19____.
3. To transact such other business as may properly come before the meeting.

(Date)   _____
                                                          Secretary

FORM 15: Waiver of Notice of Meeting of Stockholders

We, the undersigned stockholders of _____, a corporation organized and existing under the laws of the State of_____, each entitled to vote the number of shares set opposite his name, do hereby waive notice of a _____ meeting of the stockholders of the said corporation at [time] on [date] at [address], for the purpose of _____.

This waiver of notice of meeting shall be filed with the corporate books and records and made a part of the minutes of the meeting.

(Date)

Stockholder	Number of Shares
_____	_____
_____	_____
_____	_____

FORM 16: Proxy

I, _____, do hereby constitute and appoint _____ as attorney and agent for me, and in my name, place, and stead, to vote as my proxy at any stockholders' meetings to be held between the date of this proxy and _____, 19 ___, unless sooner revoked, with full power to cast the number of votes that all my shares of stock in _____ should entitle me to cast as if I were then personally present, and authorize __ _____ to act for me and in my name and stead as fully as I could act if I were present, giving to _____, attorney and agent, full power of substitution and revocation.

In witness whereof, I have executed this proxy on ___, 19 ___.

_____
Stockholder

FORM 17: Resignation of Officers and Directors

We, the undersigned, hereby tender our resignations as officers and directors of _____ to take effect immediately.

(Date)   (Signatures)

FORM 18: Minutes of Annual Meeting of Stockholders

The annual meeting of the stockholders of the corporation was held at [time] on [date] at [address].

The meeting was called to order by_____, the president of the corporation.

The secretary then reported that the meeting had been called pursuant to a notice of meeting [or waiver of notice] thereof in accordance with the bylaws. It was ordered that a copy of the notice and waiver of notice be appended to the minutes of the meeting.

The secretary then read the roll of stockholders from the stock transfer ledger. The following stockholders were present in person or by proxy:

Stockholder	Shares	In Person	By Proxy

The chairman stated that a majority of the total number of shares issued and outstanding was represented and that the meeting was complete and ready to transact any business before it. It was ordered that proxies be appended to the minutes of the meeting.

The president then gave a general report of the business and finances of the corporation and the secretary reported the following changes of stockholders since the last such report:

_____ .

The chairman then stated that the election of directors of the corporation was now in order. The following were nominated as directors: _____
_____ .

A ballot was taken, the vote was canvassed and the forego-ing nominees were duly elected directors of the corporation to serve until the next annual meeting of stockholders or until their successors are elected.

The following action was taken at the meeting: _____.

There being no further business, the meeting was, on mo-tion, adjourned.

(Date)

_____
Secretary

Ratification: We, the undersigned shareholders, or assignees thereof, have read the minutes and do hereby approve, ratify, and confirm all business transacted as reported herein.

(Signatures)

The following have been appended to the minutes: ____
_____ .

Legal Principles Governing Corporations

For most purposes, a corporation is an entity distinct from its individual members or stockholders who, as natural persons, are merged in the corporate identity. The corporation's identity remains unchanged and unaffected by changes in its individual membership. By the very nature of a corporation, its property is vested in the corporation itself and not the stockholders. The stockholders, as such, do not have the power to represent the corporation or act for it in relation to its ordinary business, nor ordinarily are they personally liable for the acts and obligations of the corporation. In no legal sense can the business of a corporation be said to be that of its individual stockholders or officers. The corporate entity is distinct even if all or a majority of its stock is owned by a single individual or corporation, or if the corporation is a *"close"* or *"family"* corporation. Thus, the ownership of all shares of stock of a corporation by one individual does not avoid the separate identity between the corporation and the individual.

These legal rules are subject to the important exception that, since the rules are for the purpose of convenience and to serve the ends of justice, the courts will, in pursuing those ends, treat the stockholders or officers as identical. In other words, the courts will pierce the fiction of, or ignore, the cor-

porate entity where justice requires it. A clear and lucid statement of the rule as currently applied by the courts is:

> When the concept of the corporate entity is employed to
> defraud creditors, to evade an existing obligation, to cir-
> cumvent a statute, to achieve or perpetuate monopoly,
> or to protect knavery or crime, the courts will draw aside
> the web of the corporate entity, and will regard the cor-
> poration as a sham, subterfuge or a fraud on the law, and
> will deal with the parties as individuals and will do justice
> between real persons.

In these situations each individual defrauded may sue the
directors, officers or other participants. Stated in realistic and
practical terms, the separate entity rule applies to honest,
"good faith" transactions, but courts will not permit dishonest
persons to use a corporate entity to avoid the obligations arising from their personal, wrongful activities. This rule is
discussed in more detail later.

Incorporation and Organization

No corporation can exist without the consent or grant of
the sovereign, or the State. The power to create corporations
is one of the attributes of sovereignty. This power is a
legislative function, and laws, rules, regulations, and procedures for creating a corporation are established by the
legislature through the enactment of statutes. Implementa-
tion of these procedures is a function of the executive branch
of the state and is usually delegated to the office of the
secretary of state or some other administrative officer. The
federal government has the power to create corporations, but
those laws are not applicable to our discussions.

Corporate Purposes

Most statutes provide for the formation of a corporation for
any lawful business purpose or purposes. Naturally, one may
not legally form a corporation and use it for the purpose of

conducting illegal activities or other purposes contrary to the laws. However, a corporation may be legally organized for the specific purpose and intent of escaping or limiting personal liability of the individual, or avoiding taxes. In fact, these are the primary purposes for forming private corporations. An honest, law-abiding person may form a private corporation and carry on honest, lawful business activities and escape personal liability. A "bad faith" formation of a corporation to carry on fraudulent, dishonest, or unlawful activities will not be approved by the courts. For our purposes, we will assume honest, law-abiding intent, motives, and activities.

Incorporators and Members

Most state statutes permit a private corporation to be formed by natural persons of legal age or by corporations and other entities. The modern trend is to permit only one person to form a corporation. Some states still require more than one incorporator. While some states provide for a minimum of three directors, the trend is toward permitting one director.

Articles of Incorporation

The contents of the articles of incorporation are determined by the local statutes. Most modern statutes, based on the Model Corporation Act, require the following items in the articles:
* Name of the corporation.
* Period of duration.
* Purpose or purposes for which the corporation is being organized.
* Number, amount, description, and nature of shares of stock authorized.
* Names and addresses of officers, directors, incorporators, and resident agent. (See Form 1)

The articles of incorporation must substantially comply with the requirements of the statutes as to both the form and contents. The courts have not hesitated to declare attempted incorporations invalid for failure to do so.

The laws usually require a statement in the articles concerning the purpose or purposes for which the corporation is formed. Vague or general specifications of purposes are not sufficient. The character of a corporation is usually determined by the objective of its formation and the nature of its business as stated in its articles. The statutes usually require that the articles be signed by the incorporator(s). It is a simple matter to comply with the formal procedures set out in the statutes.

After the articles have been completed in accordance with the requirements, they must be filed in the appropriate state office. In most states the officer who files the articles performs only routine duties, and if the articles are in proper form, he or she must file them. If they are not in conformity with the statutes, he or she must refuse to file them. The officer may, of course, refuse to file articles which indicate that the purposes of the corporation are unlawful or unauthorized. All states require payment of a filing fee. This is a prerequisite for the creation of a lawful corporation.

Most state officers and their employees are cooperative and willing to assist in supplying all information needed to complete the papers required to incorporate. The secretary of state is generally an elective office, and you will find most of these elected officers eager to please you and all other voters and taxpayers.

Where Organizational Meetings May Be Held

The term "organized" or "organization" generally means the election of officers, the subscription and payment of the capital stock, the adoption of bylaws, and other steps endowing the corporation with the capacity to transact business. Under some statutes these acts must be carried out before the corporation can legally conduct business, and these acts or functions should be performed in the state of incorporation. The articles of incorporation should be accepted by the board of directors, and the first meeting held for the purpose of organizing the corporation and electing its officers within the limits of the state creating it.

Most state statutes require that notice of the organization meeting be given to the stockholders, but such a requirement is subject to waiver. They are the only persons interested in the results obtained by giving the required notice.

Subscription to, Issuance of, and Payment for Stock

When forming a corporation, some statutes require that a specific proportion of the stock, usually a minimum amount, be subscribed, and some require that a certain portion of that stock subscribed for be actually paid in. Other statutes require that the articles state the amount of paid-in capital with which the corporation will begin business. The corporation is forbidden to begin business until the amount specified is paid. Such requirements are essential and must be complied with.

Any attempt to acquire corporate life and functions by a pretentious or evasive compliance with the statute as to issue of, or payment for, stock, no matter what the papers of the corporation say upon their face, legally are considered fraudulent. A substantial compliance with the requirements is sufficient. A majority of the states have simplified the statutes and reduced the formal requirements for incorporation.

De Jure and De Facto Corporations

A *de jure* corporation is one which has been regularly created in compliance with all requirements and has the legal sanction and authority of the state behind it. It is, therefore, invulnerable to attack or legal question. You will have this kind of corporation when you follow the statutes. An association which has not complied with the statutory requirements, but which has actually operated as a corporation and held itself out to the general public as a corporation, is called a corporation *de facto*. That is, this type of corporation exists from the fact of its acting as such, though not in law or rightfully a corporation. It is an apparent corporate organization where the individual members claim it is a valid corporation, and it is acting as such, without the authoritative sanction of the law.

It is an organization with color of law (as though it had followed the law), exercising corporate rights and franchises, and that status may not be challenged by anyone except the sovereign. A corporation *de facto* is, in short, a corporation in fact.

As a general rule, a corporation *de facto* exists when there has been an attempt to comply with the statutory requirements, but some irregularity or defect in compliance has occurred; the organization holds itself out to the public as a legal corporation; and the *de facto* organization functions and operates as though it were actually a legal corporation. The reason for this rule is that if rights and franchises have been infringed upon, they are the rights and franchises of the state. Until the state questions the validity of the *de facto* corporation, the public may treat those acting as possessing and exercising the corporate powers as doing so legally. The rule is in the interest of the public and is essential to the validity of business transactions with corporations.

Corporate Existence and Franchises

A promoter is a person who initiates the incorporation and organization of a corporation, procures for it the rights and capital by which to carry out the purposes set forth in its charter, and establishes it as able to do business. He or she brings together the persons interested in the enterprise, aids in acquiring subscriptions, and sets in motion the machinery which leads to the corporation itself. Signing and verifying articles of incorporation and subscribing for stock in the proposed company does not necessarily make one a promoter; neither does forming your own corporation.

Every person acting by whatever name in the forming and establishing of a corporation at any period prior to the company's becoming fully incorporated is considered, in law, as occupying a fiduciary relationship (position of trust) toward the corporation. A promoter stands in a fiduciary relation to both the corporation as a separate, legal entity and the individual stockholders and is bound to exercise good faith in all dealings with them. Promoters must fully disclose all essential facts touching their relationship with the corporation, stockholders, officers, directors, or any other parties.

The fiduciary position of promoters requires that all of their dealings be open and fair. They will not be allowed to benefit by any secret profit or advantage which may be gained at the expense of the corporation or its members. However, this relationship does not prevent the promoters from fairly and openly doing business with the corporation at a profit. Any payment or reward offered to promoters for their services must be with a full disclosure of the facts. The custom of promoters to divide secretly among themselves a certain portion of the stock of the corporation is fraudulent.

Until articles of incorporation have been filed and approved or other essential steps are taken to bring a corporation into legal existence, a corporation has no being, franchise, or facilities. Its promoters or those bringing it into existence are in no sense identical with the corporation. They do not represent it in any relation of agency and do not have any authority to enter into preliminary contracts binding upon the corporation. It follows that a corporation cannot, before its organization, have agents, contract for itself, or be contracted with. It is, therefore, not legally liable or responsible for any contract which a promoter attempts to make prior to its organization. A promoter's contract does not, by the incorporation of the contemplated company, become the contract of the corporation. This demonstrates the importance of completing all steps necessary for incorporation before you begin operating a business as a corporation.

Courts of equity refuse to enforce a contract against a corporation made on its behalf by promoters, agents, or others unless there appears to be some sound reason for demanding its enforcement. It is, of course, perfectly proper and legal after incorporation for the new corporation to assume voluntarily those contracts made by promoters or agents. In these situations the corporation may sue upon the contract to enforce it or recover for its breach.

A promoter who makes a contract for the benefit of the corporation, before incorporation, is personally liable on it and incurs personal liability. It frequently happens that a promoter conducts the ordinary affairs of the business as a corporation before legal incorporation. In such a case, the promoter becomes personally liable on business contracts. You are cautioned to complete all legal requirements for incorporation before engaging in any business activities in the corporate name.

Corporate Name and Seal

A name is necessary to the very existence of a corporation. Each corporation must have a name by which it can be identified, function, and operate in the conduct of any legal acts or activities. The name of a corporation designates the corporation in the same manner as the name of an individual. The right to use its corporate name is one of the legal attributes of incorporation and constitutes a franchise or a privilege granted by the state. The presence or absence in a trade name of the word "company," in and of itself, has no direct bearing on the issue as to whether the association is a corporation, partnership, or other entity.

Most statutes prohibit a private corporation from using the words "bank," "insurance," "trust," and other names which may mislead the public. A corporation may adopt any name it desires, subject to the qualification that it cannot adopt or use a name already used by another. Corporations and unincorporated associations may have a property right in their names. A corporation cannot adopt a name so similar to that of another corporation, association, or firm as would result in confusion or deception. It may not use its name for the purposes of pirating the business of a competitor. A corporation cannot adopt the name of an individual where it appears that the use of such name would lead to confusion, deception to the public, or defraud others operating a business under the same name, even though the name was taken from the names of principal stockholders, promoters, or incorporators.

A corporation may use and adopt any seal or mark as its official corporate seal. Under former common law rules a corporate seal was essential for valid contracts. However, this is no longer required as a matter of law. In all business transactions and legal relationships where a natural person will be legally bound without a seal, a corporation will also be bound. For this reason it is not necessary to obtain a corporate seal, though it is usually one of the items in the corporate kit. Even though the seal is not legally necessary, the presence of the corporate seal establishes, on its face, that the instrument to which it is affixed is the act of the corporation.

Bylaws

The bylaws of a corporation govern it. They prescribe the
relationship of the rights and duties of the members to the
internal government of the corporation; establish the procedures, practices, and policies of the business operation; approve the rules for the management of the corporate affairs;
and establish the rights and duties existing among the
members. Bylaws are self-imposed rules to regulate the manner in which the corporation will function. They include all
self-made regulations of a corporation, but generally do not
bind or affect the rights of third parties. Until repealed, the
bylaws are continuing rules for the government of the corporation and its officers, their function being to regulate the transaction of the incidental business of the corporation.

Bylaws differ from corporate resolutions in that a resolution applies to a single act of the corporation while the bylaws
govern only with reference to the rules which the directors
and officers may pass for their government. Bylaws are valid
if they are reasonable and calculated to carry into effect the
objectives of the corporation. They cannot be in conflict with
the general policy of the state and federal laws.

Records and Reports

The records of a corporation include its articles of incorporation and bylaws, and minutes of its meetings, the stock books,
the books containing the account of its official activities, and
the written evidence of its contracts and business transactions.
They are the property of the corporation, not of the officers
or employees. Most state statutes require the keeping of such
books and records. Another requirement is that corporations
make periodic statements or reports to the state agency
regulating corporations.

Stockholders have a right to inspect the books and records
of corporations, subject to reasonable company regulations.
Inconvenience to the business from an inspection of its books
is no ground for a denial of the stockholder's right to examine
the records. A stockholder's right cannot be defeated by a cor-

poration's offer to purchase his shares of stock. Moreover, an offer to furnish extracts or copies from the books or to furnish annual reports will not satisfy a demand for inspection of the original records. It is easy to see that a stockholder's lawsuit or other demands of shareholders for examination of corporate books and records could result in considerable expense, inconvenience, and disruption of the business operations of a corporation. In an attempt to resolve this problem, the courts, while recognizing the fundamental right of the stockholder to examine the books and records, have placed certain restrictions upon the exercise of those rights. One of the most important of these qualifications is that before the right of inspection will be granted over the corporation's objection, an inquiry by the court will be made into the applicant's motives.

Capital and Capital Stock

There is a difference between capital and capital stock. The capital stock of a corporation is the amount of money, property, or other means authorized by its articles of incorporation and contributed, or agreed to be contributed, by the shareholders as the financial basis for the operation of the business. These contributions are usually received from the capital investment of the shareholders or through the declaration of stock dividends.

Capital is sometimes used broadly to indicate the entire assets of the corporation, regardless of their source, which is utilized for the conduct of the corporate business and for the purpose of making gains and profits. In this sense the capital belongs to the corporation, and capital stock, when issued, belongs to the stockholders. Capital may be either real or personal property, but capital stock is always personal property. The terms are frequently used interchangeably, but it is important to note the difference.

Classes of Stock

A share of stock is a unit of interest in a corporation. Even though ownership of stock does not confer title to any of the property of the corporation, it legally entitles the shareholder to an equivalent part of the property, or its proceeds, when distributed. Each share represents a distinct and undivided share or interest in the common property of the corporation. Shares of stock constitute property distinct from the capital or tangible property of the corporation and belong to different owners. The capital is the property of the corporation. You should not treat corporate property and assets as yours even though you may own all, or substantially all, of the stock of the corporation.

Common stock is the class of stock ordinarily issued without extraordinary rights or privileges, and which, in the absence of other classes of stock having superior rights, represents the complete interest in the corporation. Preferred stock has different characteristics from, and is entitled to certain preferences over, common stock. What distinguishes preferred stock is that it is entitled to a priority over other stock in the distribution of profits, being ordinarily entitled to dividends of a definite percentage or amount. Sometimes this right to a prior dividend is the only preference which is given to such stock. Upon dissolution of the corporation preferred stockholders may, by agreement, be given a preference over common stockholders in the distribution of the capital assets of a corporation. Preferred stock is sometimes thought of as an investment rather than participating ownership of a business.

Par value stock has imprinted upon its face a dollar value. The par value of a share is simply an amount fixed as the nominal value of the interest so specified. This amount likewise indicates the sum of money or value of property or services which a subscriber is represented as having contributed to the corporation in exchange for such share in its ownership. Par value and actual value of issued stock are not necessarily the same. Par value stock is also to be distinguished from non par stock, which is simply stock without any nominal or par value.

The usual practice for a small corporation is to issue only common stock. It is also recommended that you authorize the issuance of the maximum number of shares for the minimum filing fee, but that you issue only a limited number of shares in the beginning.

Subscriptions and Purchases of Shares of Corporate Stock

Subscribers of stock are those who agree to take and pay for shares of the capital stock; they agree with each other to pay the par value of the stock. Shares of stock are personal property. Therefore, most of the principles governing rights and liabilities of the parties to a contract are applicable to sales of shares of stock. You should not make any sale of stock to the general public without complying with any applicable securities regulations or making sure the transaction is exempt.

Status of Stockholders

Ordinarily, neither the general statutes nor the articles of incorporation impose any qualification as to who may be stockholders. A corporation is a legal entity distinct from the body of its stockholders, and it represents its stockholders in all matters within the scope of its powers. A stockholder does not stand in any fiduciary relation to the directors of the corporation; rather, the directors and officers of a corporation occupy a fiduciary or quasi-fiduciary relation (resembling a position of trust) to the corporation and its stockholders. One remains a stockholder in a corporation until he transfers his shares to another person or until his status is terminated by the forfeiture of his stock. Strictly speaking, a stockholder cannot resign from a corporation.

A corporation organized for profit has no power to expel a member or declare a forfeiture of his stock, even for nonpayment of its assessments. A corporation may not adopt bylaws imposing the forfeiture of stock or of other corporate interest as a penalty for its breach, unless the power to pass such bylaws is expressly granted by the articles of incorporation. Moreover, any power given to forfeit stock must be strictly construed. If any restrictions or limitations imposed by the articles of incorporation have been disregarded, the alleged act of forfeiture will be declared invalid. A stockholder has a right to contract with a corporation as a stranger, provided the contract is in good faith.

Meetings of Stockholders

Generally, the purpose of stockholders meetings is to elect directors and transact other business calling for, or requiring, the action or consent of the stockholders. For example, meetings are called for amendment of the articles of incorporation, sale or mortgage of the corporate assets, consolidation and merger, or other relevant business. Individual stockholders are bound by the action of the majority attending corporate meetings. Due notice of meetings is given. Most small corporations have few stockholders' meetings because the control usually rests with one or two people and regular, formal meetings of stockholders are of little value.

Under some statutes, at least one meeting of stockholders must be held annually and, whether or not the statute states so specifically, this requirement is usually included in the bylaws. The matter of giving notice of stockholders' meetings is now generally regulated by statutes which usually require notice to be given of the time and place of the regular, annual meeting as well as of special meetings.

Stockholders and Creditors

In the absence of a charter, constitutional, or statutory provisions to the contrary, stockholders are not liable for any of the obligations of a corporation, whatever their character and in whatever manner incurred. The corporation is an entity distinct from its members, and, therefore, its debts are not the debts of its members. It is held that stockholders, unless they participate, are not liable for the wrongful acts of corporate agents and employees. The rule is not ordinarily affected by the fact that one person owns all or most of the stock in the corporation.

Powers and Functions of Corporations

A corporation owes its existence to the will of the state. An individual has an absolute right to use, enjoy, and dispose of all his acquisitions, without any control except by the laws of the land. The individual may perform all acts and make all contracts which are not, in the eye of the law, inconsistent with the welfare of society. However, the civil rights of a corporation are very different. A corporation has only those powers which are expressly granted in its articles of incorporation or in the statutes under which it is created. The decision of what business may be carried on by a corporation must be referred to its articles of incorporation. Without this stated power to carry on a particular business, it does not exist. It is important that you specify powers and purposes in the articles of incorporation that will generally include all acts authorized by law.

Directors, Officers, and Employees

All corporations must act and contract by means of its officers, agents, and employees. They may either hold corporate offices or be agents appointed by the appropriate officials in the regular course of the corporate business. Corporations have the power to appoint agents with full power and authority to do all things necessary and proper to enter into contracts with other corporations, individuals, or other business entities.

Directors of corporations are usually stockholders. However, it is generally not necessary to be a stockholder to be eligible as a director or trustee. The board of directors represents the impersonal corporate body, and the directors are the executive representatives of the corporation. The directors are not ordinary agents in the immediate control of the stockholders. The powers of boards of directors are, in a very important sense, original and undelegated. The stockholders do not confer, nor can they revoke, those powers or create a sterilized board of directors. The law imposes the business management of a corporation on its directors, and a corporation can act only through its directors. This is entirely consistent with the principle that the corporate entity is separate and distinct from the individual owner or owners. The stockholders do not have the general management and control of the affairs of the corporation, and they are deemed to have consented to the management and control of the corporate business by the board of directors.

The directors are authorized to transact and have the power to do whatever they, as individuals, could do if the business were theirs. A usual practice within the power of the board of directors is to appoint and authorize a committee to act for the corporation in specific or particular matters. The board may grant to this committee all authority necessary to conduct the ordinary business of the corporation.

The legal principles regarding the powers and authority of an officer or agent of a corporation are basically the same as those applicable to any agent. The authority of a corporate officer, agent, or employee may be actual in the sense that it is specifically given, or it may be implied in the sense that the agent holds himself out as having authority to act.

Rights and Liabilities between Corporation and Third Parties

As a general rule, a corporation is bound by the acts of its officers or agents who are acting within the scope of their express, implied, or apparent authority. It is not always easy to determine when an agent exceeds his authority. A corporation is not bound by acts done, or declarations made, by an officer or agent who exceeds his authority. For a corporation to be bound by the acts of its officers, agents, or employees, it must be established that the corporation knew of the acts which indicated implied or apparent authority to third parties.

Dissolution

Corporations are easy to create, and they are easy to terminate or dissolve. The state gives a corporation its existence and status as an entity, and it cannot be terminated except by some act of the sovereign power by which it was created. The courts of another state do not have the power to dissolve a corporation created by the laws of your state. In the event a corporation fails to pay franchise taxes or other taxes or assessments made by the state, it may be automatically dissolved by the state. This is a forfeiture of the grant of corporate existence by failure to comply with the statutory requirements. In this instance, the secretary of state merely declares a forfeiture of the grant, and declares the corporation dissolved and at an end. By following the statute relating to dissolution of corporations, you may voluntarily dissolve your corporation. Essentially, this involves the completion of another form you file with the secretary of state in which the corporation is voluntarily dissolved and terminated.

Special Tax Tips

You may think of the corporation as a "double tax" situation: the corporation pays income taxes on earnings and then pays dividends to the stockholders who must also pay income taxes on the dividend earnings. While this is, indeed, the way the tax code works, there are still some very interesting tax advantages to forming your own corporation. The better your tax planning the better your corporation will work for you.

As a shareholder-employee of a small business corporation you will wish to consider tax planning methods and techniques which will enable you to create tax free income, that is, income which goes to the corporation and which is used for or on your behalf, but is not income taxable to you; arrange for corporate income taxes to be in the lowest possible income tax bracket; have income which is taxable to you at the lowest income tax bracket; and plan to avoid double taxation.

You must keep in mind that the tax code is usually changed every time Congress has a session. However, based upon the past history of Congress there will always be significant tax procedures that can be utilized through the use of a corporation. You may wish to obtain professional tax advice to take advantage of the tax incentives built into the tax code. Some of the most commonly used tax advantages include the following:

- S Corporation: S Corporation is a small business corporation as defined in the tax code for which an election to be taxed under Subchapter S of the Code is in effect for that year. When you incorporate you may wish to consider whether to adopt an option under the Code to have profits of the corporation flow through to stockholders to be taxed individually rather than at corporate tax rates. You merely file IRS Form 2553 in accordance with the instructions in the tax code.

- Section 1244 Stock: Under Section 1244 of the Internal Revenue Code you are permitted, under certain circumstances, to take ordinary tax loss treatment for certain stock issues.

- Separate Tax Year: By selecting a "fiscal year" for your corporation that is different from your personal tax year, you can effectively create significant deferral of income taxes.

- Ordinary and Necessary Business Expenses: This arises by virtue of the fact that many of your business expenses can result in direct benefits to you. Typically, business owners can deduct reasonable salaries as business expenses to the corporation, travel and entertainment expenses, an office at home used exclusively for business purposes, and all other expenses allowed under the tax code. The key to all legitimate deductions of such expenses is advance planning and proper records.

- Medical Reimbursement Plans: Under a medical reimbursement plan, the corporation can either reimburse an employee for all or part of the medical expenses for that employee, the employee's spouse, and other dependents or pay those expenses directly on behalf of the employee. The amounts reimbursed or paid under a qualified medical reimbursement plan are fully deductible by the corporation and not taxable income to the employee. The effect is to make medical expenses fully tax deductible. These expenses are defined more broadly than they are on a personal return. Your medical reimbursement plan should be in writing; be approved in the minutes of the corporation; set forth all the requirements that an employee must meet in order to be eligible for the plan; include what ex-

penses are covered and how and when payments are to
be made; require eligible employees to submit receipts,
canceled checks, or other evidence of medical expenses;
and exclude any expenses that are covered and otherwise
paid by insurance.

- Group Term Life Insurance: Group term life insurance
premiums are paid and deducted by the corporation. You
can name the beneficiaries of the policy. The obvious tax
advantage is that the premiums paid by the corporation
are deductible to the corporation and are not taxable income to you. Like almost all life insurance, the proceeds
received by the beneficiary upon death are income tax
free. There are certain limitations on the amounts
permitted.
- Members of Your Family on Corporate Payroll: You are
able to have your corporation hire members of your family
as employees. The two most common reasons for hiring
family members are income splitting and qualifying family
members for social security.
- Combine Business Trips With Vacations: Expenses incurred by you for attending a board meeting or other
business purposes can be paid by the corporation, and the
expenses are deductible to the corporation and are not
considered to be taxable income to you. Proper record
keeping is essential for these expenses. Of course, expenses for your personal vacation are not deductible.
- Company Car: The use of company owned automobiles and
airplanes, including all operating and maintenance expenses, used for business purposes, is deductible to the
corporation and is not taxable income to the employee.

Piercing the Corporate Veil

When the concept of the corporate entity is employed to defraud creditors, to evade an existing obligation, to circumvent a statute, to achieve or perpetuate monopoly, or to protect knavery or crime, the courts will draw aside the web of the corporate entity, and will regard the corporation as a sham, subterfuge or a fraud on the law, and will deal with the parties as individuals and will do justice between real persons. The principle of piercing the fiction of the corporate entity is, however, to be applied with great caution. While corporate entities may be disregarded where they are made the implement for legal avoidance, they will not be disregarded where those in control have deliberately adopted the corporate form in order to secure its advantages and where no legal violation is done by treating the corporate entity as a separate legal person. This is your goal. If you comply with the laws and avoid wrongdoing, you will have no difficulty with this rule.

Historical Development of the Rule

As early as 1809, it was perceived by the courts that the literal application of the notion that a corporation is only a legal entity, and nothing more, could work injustice in some situations. From its beginning, the Supreme Court of the United States had taken over the language of the old English yearbooks, and proclaiming its allegiance to them, had agreed with the early English writers that "a corporation aggregate of many is invisible, immortal, and rests only in intendment and consideration of the law." But if a corporation is merely a legal entity, if it is clothed only with invisibility and intangibility, it could not, of course, be a citizen of the state.

The federal constitution, however, limits the jurisdiction of the federal courts "to controversies between citizens of different states." In 1809, Chief Justice Marshall, in order to preserve the jurisdiction of the federal courts over corporations, was compelled to look beyond the entity "to the character of the individuals who compose the corporation." His court proclaimed that "substantially and essentially" the parties to the suit are the stockholders, and that their several state citizenships would be recognized for purposes of federal court jurisdiction.

From later cases and statutes the rule evolved that a corporation is deemed a citizen of its state of incorporation and state of its principal place of business. (See 28 U.S.C.A. 1332). Even at this early date, the U.S. Supreme Court did not regard it as reasonable that the operation of the separate corporate concept should take from the federal courts their important and far-reaching jurisdiction over corporations, a result which any overzealous adherence to the theory of corporate entity would inevitably require. From that time on, in certain cases, the courts have drawn aside the veil and looked at the character of the individual incorporators.

Rationale of Piercing the Corporate Veil Doctrine

The doctrine that a corporation is a legal entity existing separate and apart from the persons comprising it is a legal theory introduced for the purposes of convenience and to subserve the ends of justice. The entity theory provides the traditional basis for the concept of limited liability, as well as the corporation's capacity to hold property, to contract not only with outsiders but also with its own shareholders, to sue and be sued, and to enjoy continued existence notwithstanding changes in its membership. The concept cannot, however, be extended to the point beyond its reason and policy, and when invoked in support of a subversive end will be disregarded by the courts.

The basic legal proposition, the rule of law of piercing the corporate veil, may seem inconsistent with the well-established rules of separate entity. However, it is a necessary application of the legal process by the courts to protect the public. This complex and precarious rule of law and the apparent inconsistency is really a result of the courts being faced with a very tough legal problem: how to create, by a legal fiction, the separate entity of a corporation, and at the same time prevent persons from using the device to do wrong.

Application of the Rule of Piercing the Corporate Veil

Even though the rule is stated in all-inclusive language covering six general categories of cases, you must remember that cases come in all colors, shapes, forms, and varied factual situations. One court made the following observation about the rule:

> *The general rules of law with respect to the piercing of the corporate veil and disregarding the corporate entity are well-established, but they offer very little aid when it comes to the decision of a particular case. The decisions are framed in broad principles and there are various theories used to justify the piercing.* (National Bond Finance Co. v. General Motors Corp., 238 F.S. 248, affirmed 341 F 2d 1022)

The six general categories of cases in which the courts will disregard the corporate entity are:
- Where the fiction is used to promote a fraud;
- Where the corporate fiction is resorted to as a means of evading an existing legal obligation;
- Where the corporate fiction is employed to achieve or promote a monopoly;
- Where the corporate fiction is used to circumvent a statute;
- Where the corporate fiction is relied upon as a protection of crime or to justify wrong;
- Where a corporation is organized and operated as a mere tool or business conduit of another corporation.

Insofar as you are personally concerned there are certain telling signs that courts look for in assisting them to determine the status of any particular case:

- Where the stockholders ignore the existence of the corporation, for example, failure to hold meetings, failure to record minutes, etc.
- Where the stockholders ignore the existence of the corporation, for example, by mixing personal and corporate funds or by dealing with the corporation's customers as if they were the stockholder's customers; or treating the corporate debts and income as their own.
- Where the corporation is inadequately financed, for example, where the stockholders do not contribute enough capital so that there is a reasonable likelihood that the corporation can pay its debts.

The mechanical application of some legal formula in determining if the corporation invalid is inherently dangerous. As a practical matter, because of the ingenuity and imagination of the American business owner, there is no general formula to fit all cases. The courts are faced with the same problem as the Congress in its attempts to close tax loopholes. As soon as one tax loophole is closed the American taxpayers think up two new ones. Under these circumstances the courts frequently say that each situation must be considered by the courts on its own merits. That is a wide range of booby traps. In order to give you a better picture of the rules, we will discuss the general categories of cases and give selected, leading cases to illustrate the actions taken by the courts.

Fraud

Fraud is defined as an intentional perversion of the truth for the purpose of inducing another in reliance upon it to part with some valuable thing belonging to him or to surrender a legal right; a false representation of a matter of fact, whether by words or by conduct, by false or misleading allegations, or by concealment of that which should have been disclosed, which deceives and is intended to deceive another so that he shall act upon it to his legal injury; or any kind of artifice employed by one person to deceive another. Bad faith and fraud are sometimes used interchangeably.

Although the term fraud or fraudulent is used to designate a general class of cases in which the corporate veil will be lifted, you should understand that fraud is liberally sprinkled over many of the cases in other categories. Fraud and bad faith will trigger courts to come down heavy in all sorts of cases.

Avoiding Legal Obligations

The earliest recorded history of mankind reflects a strong, natural desire, an ineluctable urge, an obsession, for individual upmanship. Just as soon as the concept of a corporation, the separate entity idea, developed, there were immediately those who exercised the natural instinct to hide behind the corporate veil as a cloak to cheat others and swindle creditors. In appropriate cases, courts were quick in taking care of this problem.

Achieve or Promote a Monopoly

In cases involving an attempt to monopolize, it has become necessary, from a just and practical standpoint, to look behind the corporate body and recognize the individual members. The leading case, and one of the most famous of these holdings, is *People v. North River Sugar Refining Co., 121 N.Y. 582.* Proceedings were brought against the company by the state of New York to deprive it of its corporate franchise for the reason that it had abused its rights and obligations by becoming a party to a forbidden and wholly illegal trust agreement. The corporation insisted that it had never entered into the contract, but it appeared that the contract was signed by each

and every shareholder. It was strenuously argued by counsel
that the agreements were those only of the individual
shareholders in their private capacities and with regard to
their private property, and hence not corporate action of
misconduct. It was contended that the absence of any formal
action by the directors of the corporation proved that it, the
entity, was free from guilt. It was urged that the illegal combination was the result merely of dealings of the stockholders
and not of any corporate action and that, therefore, the entity
was not chargeable with any wrongdoing or misbehavior.

The Court of Appeals affirmed the judgment of dissolution
rendered in the court below and charged the entity with the
acts of the stockholders and officers, deciding that under the
circumstances of the case, their acts were the acts of the corporation itself. The court pointed out the utter ridiculousness
of the appellant's argument that "while all that was human
and could act had sinned, yet the impalpable entity had not
acted at all and must go free."

The court ignored the corporate concept, brushed aside the
entity and did not hesitate to "look beneath it at the actions
of the individuals upon whom the franchise was conferred."
The court said:

> *The State gave the franchise, the charter, not to the im-*
> *palpable, intangible and almost nebulous fiction of our*
> *thought, but to the corporators, the individuals, and act-*
> *ing and living men, to be used by them, to redound to*
> *their benefit, to strengthen their hand, and add energy*
> *to their capital. ... The benefit is theirs, the punishment*
> *is theirs, and both must attend and depend upon their*
> *conduct; and when they all act, collectively, as an ag-*
> *gregate body, without the least exception, and so acting,*
> *reach results and accomplish purposes clearly corporate*
> *in their character, and affecting the vitality, the in-*
> *dependence, the utility, of the corporation itself, we can-*
> *not hesitate to conclude that there has been corporate*
> *conduct which the state may review, and not be defeated*
> *by the assumed innocence of a convenient fiction.*

Circumvent a Statute

Frequently the corporate form of organization is adopted in order to evade a statute or to modify its intent. A good example is *U.S. v. Lehigh Valley R.R. Co. 220 U.S. 257*, in which the court disregarded the theory of corporate entity in enforcing the commodities clause of the Hepburn Act. The commodities clause provided:

> *It shall be unlawful for any railroad company to transport from any State... to any other State... any article... manufactured, mined or produced by it, or under its authority, or which it may own in whole or in part, or in which it may have any interest direct or indirect.*

In the first suit, the government alleged that Lehigh Valley owned stock in a coal company whose goods it was carrying. It was held that no violation of the statute was thereby shown. The court interpreted "interest direct or indirect" as meaning only a legal or equitable interest in the transported articles. The government filed an amended complaint in which it was set forth, in addition to the allegations of the prior complaint, that the railroad company was using the coal company merely as a sham in order to evade the provisions of the federal act. The court held that no such evasion could succeed, and disregarding the corporate concept and looking at the substance and reality of things, decided that it was within its jurisdiction to issue an injunction. Many attempts have been made to make the same or similar maneuvers.

Protection of Crime or to Justify Wrong

If you commit any crime or wrong under the guise of a corporate entity, you may be held personally responsible because the courts will simply look beyond the corporate veil. We have all heard of the guy who burned down the building, or otherwise had a fire, and had his corporation file a claim against the fire insurance company. In a leading case the court affirmed a criminal conviction for embezzlement, the court saying:

> *One can convert the money to his own use by putting it into the treasury and mingling it with the funds of an insolvent corporation, which is under his control and management, and of which he is a stockholder and officer in charge... It is paid into that which is a mere instrumentality created by him under sanction of law, but as much under his control and as subservient to his will as the furniture of his office or the books of account in which he records his transactions. Under such circumstances, there is no room for legal fiction of separate corporate personality, or for distinction between the defendant's acts as officer of the corporation and his acts as an independent natural person.* (Milbrath v. State, 138 Wis 354, 120 N.W. 252).

Parent, Subsidiary or Affiliated Corporations; Common Ownership of Separate Corporations

It is a generally accepted rule that the mere fact that one corporation owns all or a majority of the stock of another corporation does not destroy the identity of the second corporation as a separate legal entity. Conversely, a holding company or parent corporation has a separate corporate existence and is to be treated as a separate entity, in the absence of circumstances justifying disregard of the corporate entity. Subsidiary corporations are also separate and independent entities as a general rule.

The fact that stockholders or officers in two corporations may be the same persons does not operate to destroy the legal identity of either corporation. Even where one corporation exercises a controlling influence over another through the ownership of its stock or through the identity of stockholders, the separate entity concept, standing alone, is not affected.

Separate corporate existence of parent and subsidiary or affiliated corporations will not be recognized where one corporation is so organized and controlled and its business conducted in such a manner as to make it merely an agency, instrumentality, adjunct, or alter ego of another corporation. Just as in the case of individuals, the function of the separate corporate identity of two corporations will not be extended to permit one of the corporations to evade its obligations, to promote fraud or illegality, or to result in injustice.

Judge Cardozo in his now famous "mists of metaphor" comment, said:

> *The whole problem of the relation between parent and subsidiary corporations is one that is still enveloped in the mists of metaphor. Metaphors in law are to be narrowly watched, for starting as devices to liberate thought, they end often by enslaving it. We say at times that the corporate entity will be ignored when the parent corporation operates a business through a subsidiary which is characterized as an "alias" or a "dummy." All this is well enough if the picturesqueness of the epithets does not lead us to forget that the essential term to be defined is the act of operation. Dominion may be so complete, interference so obtrusive, that by the general rules of agency the parent will be a principal and the subsidiary an agent. Where control is less than this, we are remitted to the tests of honesty and justice ... The logical consistency of a juridical conception will indeed be sacrificed at times, when the sacrifice is essential to the end that some accepted public policy may be defended or upheld. This is so, for illustration, though agency in any proper sense is lacking, where the attempted separation between parent and subsidiary will work a fraud upon the law. ... At such times unity is ascribed to parts which, at least for many purposes, retain an independent life, for the*

reason that only thus can we overcome a perversion of the privilege to do business in a corporate form (Berkey v. Third Ave. Ry Co., 244 N.Y. 84, 155 N.E. 58).

The courts have applied various theories, rules, and reasoning to the principle, but the fact that the parent has control over the subsidiary by virtue of stock ownership is basic to the concept of the parent-subsidiary relationship. The net result of the application of most of the theories is a determination of the degree of respect which corporate formalities have been given. Ideally, determination of parental liability based on given facts should be an objective process, but there frequently is ample space for divergent judgments. We simply have to keep asking the jury or judge in each factual situation to make a final decision.

The Foreign Corporation: Doing Business in Other States

We have already discussed the economic and legal hazards, among other disadvantages, of your forming a corporation in a foreign forum — another state or country — to operate business activities in your own state. The additional expenses, very substantial in most cases, and the potential exposure to personal and corporate liabilities are all totally unnecessary. Moreover, you would be unduly complicating a very simple procedure of incorporation.

There are many problems you should know about in operating as a foreign corporation, whether it is a foreign corporation doing business in your state or your domestic corporation doing business in another state. These include:

- Statutory qualifications, procedures and requirements along with the attendant expenses;
- Civil and criminal penalties for failure to comply;
- Potential fines and personal liabilities;
- Exposure to service of process in another state;
- Potential taxation hazards.

After reviewing these items, if you still want a foreign corporation I strongly recommend you get good legal advice from a competent lawyer. If you have some "secret" activities or

clandestine operations which impel you to foreign forum shopping, I would suggest you go to the offshore islands.

The following discussions will be confined to the legal principles of law involved in a foreign corporation qualifying in
states where it does business; the exposure to service of process in other states; the exposure to taxation in other states;
and the exposure to personal liability and criminal penalties
of officers, directors, or agents who fail to comply with statutory qualification procedures by foreign corporations. But this
is only the foreign corporation gambit. If you form your own
corporation in your own state and are not *doing business* in
some other state or country you don't have to bother about
these sticky questions.

What Is "Doing Business" in Another State?

All corporate directors, officers, agents, and employees
should know the ever present potential liabilities and penalties
of doing business in another state without qualification in that
state. It doesn't matter whether your corporation is doing
business in another state or a foreign corporation does business
with you, or your corporation, in your state. It works both
ways. If you slip up, it may be costly to you; if the other guy
slips up in your state you may have a great advantage over
him in any dispute or lawsuit. In all events it is vital to know
about the responsibilities imposed by the law on corporate
officials.

A corporation is, for most purposes, a citizen of the state
of incorporation. Although a corporation has the capacity to
exercise its powers in other states, it has no inherent right
to exist or do business there without first getting permission
from that state. Each state has a legitimate purpose and motive
in exercising the power to exclude or restrict foreign corporations based on public policy, and the protection of its residents.
But this general rule is subject to certain qualifications. The
Interstate Commerce Clause, the Due Process Clause, Equal
Privileges and Immunities Clause, and the Equal Protection
of the Law Clauses of the United States Constitution grants
certain fundamental rights to citizens and persons which cannot be abridged by the several states.

When a corporation does business outside of the state in which it is organized, it may be required to *qualify*. That is, it must obtain a certificate of authority and appoint a resident agent upon whom process may be served, and take any other steps required by statutes. The corporation laws of all of the states require qualification of foreign corporations. Although there is no comprehensive definition of the term *doing business* that will answer all questions that may arise, it is important for you to know about the meaning of the phrase *doing business* as that term is used by the courts.

In all states, unqualified foreign corporations doing intrastate business are denied access to the courts and may therefore be unable to enforce contracts or collect debts in the state. Some foreign corporations, because of the potential liability, take precautions by qualifying even when there is doubt as to whether or not they are required to do so. Some corporate officials are unaware of the extent to which their corporations may be doing business in another state. Failure to qualify may subject a foreign corporation to fines. In several states, directors, officers, and agents of such corporations may be fined or even imprisoned; or may be held personally liable on contracts entered into in the state by the corporation.

The concept of *doing business* in a foreign state generally arises in three contexts: qualification, service of process (Long Arm Statutes), and taxation.

One court, in describing the situation, stated that:

> *The three general types of doing business have reference to the question before the court, i.e., whether the foreign corporation is subject to the state's taxing jurisdiction, whether it is subject to the process of the court within the state and whether or not it has subjected itself to the regulatory or qualification statutes of the state depend to a greater or less extent on the amount of activity of the corporation within the state. . . . This much seems to be clear that the greatest amount of business activity is required to subject a corporation to the state's statutory qualification requirements.* (Filmakers Releasing Organ v. Realart, 374 S.W. 2d 335).

Recent decisions of the United States Supreme Court and
the language of the state statutes have eroded the struggle
over the term *doing business* to the point where the slightest
activity can subject your corporation to the jurisdiction of the
foreign state. The starting point in understanding the laws
relative to the doing business concept is, first, the language
of the state statutes in question; second, the constitutional
limitations imposed by the federal constitution; and, third, the
interpretations placed on the statutes by the court. One classic
statement is:

> *It is established by well considered general authorities
> that a foreign corporation is doing, transacting, carrying
> on, or engaging in business within a state when it trans-
> acts some substantial part of its ordinary business
> therein.* (Royal Insurance Co., v. All States Theatres, 6
> So 2d 494).

Doing business is really not subject to a precise definition,
but depends upon the particular facts and circumstances of
each case. It is almost like saying it is a jury question. It is
a fact issue to be decided in each case on the evidence. The
cumulative facts, the totality of the corporate activities, are
the controlling criteria upon which the court decisions are
based.

Frequently courts are presented with the question of the
necessity of qualifying when an out of state corporation files
a lawsuit against a local party who raises as a defense the
assertion that the foreign corporation failed to qualify under
the state statutes and therefore cannot, under the statute, have
access to the courts of the state. The court then must determine whether the unlicensed foreign corporation was in fact
doing business in the state in violation of the statute.

This can be a shocking, embarrassing, and expensive ex-
perience for corporate officers. If your corporation is doing
business in another state, or if it might later be doing business
in another state, for any of the purposes mentioned above, you
should take a look at the statutes of the states in question and
take whatever steps may be necessary to comply with the laws.

Qualification

Qualification is easier to define. It is the process by which a foreign corporation signifies its presence in the state and by which it submits itself to the laws and conditions of admission to do business in the state as legally prescribed. This process generally consists of the filing of the documents specified by the statutes and state regulations which usually includes an application for admission, the designation of an agent upon whom service of process may be made, and the payment of an admission fee. It is about the same as filing the papers to form your corporation in your own state, but more expensive. It is just as simple; you don't need a lawyer to do it.

Technically, the *qualification* means the fulfilling of any act required by the state statute which is requisite to have the foreign corporation officially submit itself to the state's jurisdiction. Penalties are imposed for lack of proper compliance. Qualification may also include establishing the principal place of business in the state, keeping books in the state, and filing statements of financial condition. Again, these are much like the requirements of your own state where you incorporated. There are certain limitations on the scope of these statutes imposed by the Interstate Commerce Clause and the Due Process Clause of the Federal Constitution, but these have almost been taken away in a flood of judicial decisions favorable to governmental control of business operations.

The question is frequently presented as to just what activities in another state constitutes doing business so as to require corporation compliance with the qualification statutes. Generally more business activity is required to generate the necessity for qualification than for other purposes such as taxation, process, and regulation.

A corporation which is engaged exclusively in interstate commerce—and not intrastate business—need not qualify. This would be an undue burden on commerce within the meaning of the Interstate Commerce Clause of the Federal Constitution.

Many of the state statutes are explicit about what activities do, or do not, constitute doing business and just what activities

will require a foreign corporation to qualify in the state. The
necessity of qualification and the Commerce Clause of the U.S.
Constitution are inextricably intertwined. Qualification
statutes, by their nature, are regulatory and cannot be imposed
on corporations engaged exclusively in interstate commerce
without denying such corporations the protection afforded interstate commerce by the Commerce Clause. The immunity
of corporations engaged exclusively in interstate commerce
from such regulatory statutes was restated by the U.S.
Supreme Court in *Eli Lilly and Company v. Sav-On Drugs,
Inc., 366 U.S. 276 (1961)*:

> *It is well established that New Jersey cannot require
> Lilly to get a certificate of authority to do business in
> the State if its participation in this trade is limited to
> its wholly interstate sales to New Jersey wholesalers.
> .. it is equally well settled that if Lilly is engaged in in-
> trastate as well as interstate aspects of the New Jersey
> drug business, the State can require it to get a certificate
> of authority to do business.*

Service of Process: Long Arm Statutes

Service of process on an unlicensed foreign corporation turns
on the contacts with the state and on traditional notions of
fair play and substantial justice. The legal arguments gener-
ated by the legal issue as to whether the courts of one state
can exercise *in personam* jurisdiction over persons residing
in another state or a foreign corporation has been one of the
most challenging, changing, and momentous issues in our legal
system. Can a person living in Los Angeles, for example, sue
a person who lives in Miami, Florida, in the Superior Court
in Los Angeles thereby requiring him to go to court in California? If so, under what circumstances? Or can a resident of
Plains, Georgia, sue a resident of Fairbanks, Alaska, in the
local courts of Georgia? Can your corporation get sued in the
courts of New York? Or Wyoming? The legality, constitu-
tionality, and the fairness of these situations and others are
extremely important to you and your corporation.

Three of the leading U.S. Supreme Court cases on this issue are *International Shoe Co. v. Washington, 326 U.S. 310 (1945); McGee v. International Life Insurance Co., 355 U.S. 220 (1957);* and *Hanson v. Danckla, 357 U.S. 235 (1958).* The courts have generally stated the rules established by the U.S. Supreme Court on the issues as follows:

Rule 1: The nonresident defendant must do some act or consummate some transaction within the forum. It is not necessary that the defendant's agent be physically within the forum, for this act or transaction may be by mail only. A single event will suffice if its effects within the state are substantial enough to qualify under Rule Three.

Rule 2: The cause of action must be one which arises out of, or results from, the activities of the defendant within the forum. It is conceivable that the actual cause of action might come to fruition in another state, but because of the activities of defendant in the forum state there would still be *substantial minimum contact.*

Rule 3: Having established by Rules One and Two a minimum contact between the defendant and the state, the assumption of jurisdiction based upon such contact must be consonant with the due process tenants of *fair play* and *substantial justice.* If this test is fulfilled, there exists a *substantial minimum contact* between the forum and the defendant. The reasonableness of subjecting the defendant to jurisdiction under this rule is frequently tested by standards analogous to those of *forum non conveniens.*

Taxation

The right of a state to tax the activities of a foreign corporation is limited by Article I, Section 8 of the U.S. Constitution which states that, "The Congress shall have power ... to regulate Commerce ... among the several states." The con-

stitution doesn't bar a state from taxing a foreign corporation
for the privilege of doing intrastate business, nor from taxing the income of a foreign corporation derived from its intrastate business, even though it may also be doing an interstate business. But, can a state tax the exclusively interstate activities of a foreign corporation?

A federal statute, *15 U.S.C. 381*, prohibits states and political
subdivisions from imposing a net income tax on income derived
within the state from interstate commerce where the activities
of the taxpayer in the state are limited to the solicitation of
orders.

The purpose of the statute was to clarify certain aspects
of the intent of the Interstate Commerce Clause of the U.S.
Constitution. One court said:

> ... *"solicitation" should be limited to those generally ac-
> cepted or customary acts in the industry which lead to
> the placing of orders, not those who follow as a natural
> result of the transaction, such as collections, servicing
> complaints, technical assistance and training.*

In most cases one of the underlying questions is whether
the activities of the foreign corporation are sufficient to constitute the doing of instrastate business so as to remove the
corporation from the protection of the Interstate Commerce
Clause. Many court decisions have weighed the significance,
alone and cumulatively, of various business activities. Some
activities have been universally held to constitute *doing
business*, such as maintaining a stock of goods in a state from
which deliveries are regularly made to customers in that state.
Other activities, standing alone, have been held to fall short
of doing business. The mere solicitation of orders, or the
maintenance of an office in furtherance of the interstate activities of the corporation is not sufficient activity in the state
to warrant imposition of taxes. Some of the leading cases on
this issue include: *National Geographic Society v. California
Board of Equalization, 97 S.Ct 1386; Complete Auto Transit,
Inc. v. Brady, 97 S.Ct 1076; Piper v. Chris-Craft Industries,
Inc., 97 S.Ct 926;* and *Santa Fe Industries, Inc. v. Green, 97
S.Ct 1292.*

How To Prepare Your Own Partnership Agreement

PART II

Introduction

If you are one of the many people considering the formation of a business partnership this section will give you all the information you need.

It is very easy and inexpensive to establish a partnership. In fact, it can be done with nothing more than a handshake and a vague, general understanding that the partners will work together in a business venture with the hope and expectation of making money. However, the ease of entering into a partnership should not mislead you. There can be unexpected consequences. Serious legal responsibilities and liabilities are involved in becoming a partner in any business organization. The fact that you may have full and complete trust and confidence in your partner does not safeguard you from legal liabilities. I will warn you about these potential liabilities you assume as a partner.

Knowing about the liabilities of partnerships is important but you should also know your partners. No matter how well you know your prospective partner or partners, no matter how honest and understanding they may be, you should prepare your agreement in a businesslike way at the outset to avoid misunderstandings and legal entanglements later.

This section contains all the basic forms as well as a complete checklist of items to consider in preparing your partnership agreement. A partnership is not only a legal relationship, it is also a personal relationship or status. Before entering into a partnership, the people involved generally should consider the advantages and disadvantages of this type of business organization as compared to those of the corporation or others. The information in this book will enable you to make a sound comparison.

Benjamin Franklin once said:

> *Partnerships often finish in quarrels; but I was happy in this, that mine were all carried on and ended amicably, owing I think, a good deal to the precaution of having very explicitly settled in our articles everything to be done by, or expected from each partner, so there was nothing to dispute, which precaution I would therefore recommend to all who enter into partnerships.*

The Uniform Partnership Act defines a partnership as an association of two or more persons to carry on as co-owners a business for profit. A more complete definition is:

> *A partnership is a contract of two or more competent persons to place their money, effects, labor, and skill in lawful commerce or business, and to divide the profit and bear the loss in certain proportions; it is a contractual relationship between individuals in which the members ordinarily possess the power to do, in business, what individuals can and usually do in such business, except as specifically limited by the partnership contract or denied by law.*

To state that partners are co-owners of a business means each has the power of ultimate control. To determine if a particular association is a partnership, the test is whether the parties, acting in good faith and with a business purpose, intend to join together to conduct the enterprise. All the facts must be considered: the agreement, the conduct of the parties in carrying out its provisions, their statements, the testimony of disinterested persons, the relationship of the parties, their respective abilities and capital contributions, the sharing of profits and losses, the actual control of the business, and any other facts highlighting the true intent of the parties. When employed, this test presents a difficult problem particularly if the parties want to share the profits but not the losses, or if they want to share the income but not the control.

Frequently, people want the benefits of a partnership, but not the liabilities. In the development of the laws of partnership in England from 1600 to 1850 it was held that the receipt by a person of a share of the profits of the business was enough to make him a partner; but this objective test, easy to apply, was soon rejected as unworkable. Sharing profits is, indeed, a very important factor. For example, the Uniform Partnership Act that it is *prima facie* evidence that the person receiving a share of the profits is a partner in the business except where the profits are received as payment for a debt, wages, rent, annuit to a widow or representative of a deceased partner, interest on a loan, or as the consideration for the sale of good will.

On the other hand, a limited partnership is one in which the liability of some members, but not all, is limited. Such a partnership may be formed under most state statutes which permit an individual to contribute a specific sum of money to the capital of a partnership and limit his liability for losses to that amount. The partnership must otherwise comply with the requirements of the statute.

For income tax purposes, the term *partnership* includes a syndicate, group, pool, joint venture, or other unincorporated organization through or by means of which any business, financial operation, or venture is carried on, and which is not a corporation or a trust or estate. This definition obviously expands the meaning of partnership under the definitions given above, but only for tax purposes.

A partnership as an entity is not subject to the income tax. It must file an annual return (Form 1065K-1, with a copy to each partner) stating specifically the items of its gross income and allowable deductions, but this return is for information purposes only and no payment is required. In general, the taxable income of a partnership is computed in the same manner as in the case of an individual, except that income and loss must be itemized according to derivation, and certain deductions are not allowed.

The individual partners are liable for the payment of income tax. Each partner reports the tax due on his share of partnership income on his or her own individual return. A partner's share of partnership income is generally determined by the partnership agreement.

A family partnership is one whose members are closely related by blood or marriage. Family partnerships are sometimes created to shift income from the organizer of a business to members of his or her family. This reduces the family taxes if the family members are in lower tax brackets. Although tax savings is sometimes the only motive for the partnership, the Internal Revenue Service will recognize the arrangement if, after IRS investigation, the family members are found to actually own their partnership interests. This depends on the intent of the parties, determined from all the facts — the agreement, the relationship of the parties, their conduct, statements, individual abilities and capital contributions, who controls the income and how it is used, and any other facts showing their true intent.

In your consideration of a partnership as a business entity you should keep in mind that you are exposed to personal liability in all business transactions. Knowing this you should be very careful in the selection of your partners. In tax matters the question of whether a partnership exists will depend on the definitions set out in the Internal Revenue Code.

The Laws of Partnerships

The business relationship known as partnership already existed when the Code of Hammurabi and the Mosaic law were being formulated. Partnership law today rests, in part, on the common law, but was developed in England from the civil law and from the law merchant. Partnership matters were decided in special mercantile courts, such as the Courts of Staple which received parliamentary sanction in England in 1353. But it was not until the middle of the eighteenth century, under Lord Mansfield, that the common law began to develop its commercial law. Although the use of the partnership form of business organization became widespread in the nineteenth century, there was considerable confusion as to the applicable law, which was a combination of the law merchant and the common law.

Prior to the development of the common law of England the law merchant or "The Law of Merchants" had a profound influence on the laws of partnership. The law merchant has been described as follows:

It may be defined as a number of usages, each of which exist among merchants and persons engaged in mercantile transactions, not only in one particular country, but throughout the civilized world, and each of which has acquired such notoriety, not only amongst those persons,

*but also in the mercantile world at large, that the Courts
of this country will take judicial notice of it. A usage of
the law merchant has therefore two characteristics—it
must in the first place amount to* jus gentium, *that is to
say, it must be in vogue beyond the limits of this country and its notoriety must be cosmopolitan rather than
national; and in the second place it must be of such a
nature that it will receive judicial notice in our Courts.
It does not follow, however, that every mercantile usage
of which the Courts take judicial notice forms a part of
the law merchant. It is composed of those usages of merchants and traders in the different departments of trade
which have been ratified by the decisions of Courts of
law and adopted as settled law with a view to the interests of trade and the public convenience.* (Halsbury's
Laws of England, 2nd ed., 1933.)

In England, the Partnership Act of 1890 was enacted to
codify the existing law on the subject while in the United
States attempts were made in several states to codify the law
on partnership.

The Uniform Partnership Act

The Uniform Partnership Act was approved in 1914 by the
National Conference of Commissioners on Uniform State Laws.
It has now been adopted, in whole or in part, in virtually all
states. The basic purpose of the Uniform Act is to draft
statutes governing the commercial law in clear, simple terms
that can be utilized by all of the states. This promotes uniformity and stability in business law. The Act makes new rules in
some areas, such as in the provision for regulating the
priorities for liability of a partner's interest, and for new property status called tenancy in partnership. The Act does not
contain all the law affecting partnerships. The question of
capacity to become partners is generally decided on common
law principles. Suits by and against partnerships in the firm
name and service of process are generally subjects of special
statutory regulations. Although most of the state statutes are

patterned after this Act, they are not all identical. Therefore, when you have a specific question, check the wording of your state statutes. Limited partnerships, discussed later, are the subject of another uniform act.

Definition and Description of Partnerships

As mentioned in the introduction, the widely accepted definition of a partnership is, according to the Uniform Partnership Act, "an association of two or more persons to carry on as co-owners a business for profit." Draftsmen of the act recognized that it is neither practical nor feasible to frame an exact and comprehensive definition of a partnership. This is partly because partnerships resemble and have certain features or characteristics in common with, various other groups, associations, transactions, or relationships. These distinctions are explained later to give you an understanding of the many situations in which you could unknowingly become a partner.

A more inclusive definition, based upon the historical development of partnerships, is that a partnership is a contract, express or implied, between two or more competent persons to place their money, effects, labor, or skill, or some or all of them into business, and to divide the profits and bear the losses in certain proportions. These definitions can be better understood and more easily applied when we recognize the essential criteria, tests, or indicia of partnerships.

When the courts are presented with the question as to whether a partnership exists in specific fact situations, they generally look for four essentials:
• Two or more parties intending to be partners,
• Sharing of profits and losses,
• Joint ownership and control of capital assets or property of the group, and
• Joint control and management of the business.

The two main types of partnerships are general and limited. General partnerships are further classified in some states as trading, or commercial, partnerships, and nontrading, or ordinary, partnerships. A limited partnership can be formed only by compliance with the statutory requirements.

A trading partnership is one engaged in the business of buying or selling for profit; any other partnership business is called a nontrading partnership. Nontrading partnerships include business or professional activities among attorneys, physicians, contractors, builders, farmers, plumbers, real estate brokers, insurance agents, and other service businesses or professions. Recent statutory enactments in some states authorize certain professional groups to form special professional corporations. These professional corporations are not partnerships. You should not attempt to form these without professional advice.

A dormant partner, also known as a secret or silent partner, is generally one whose name is not used by the firm, and who is generally unknown to those dealing with the partnership. This is a person whose connection with the partnership business is concealed and does not usually take any active part in the business. Silent partners have the same general powers as ordinary partners and have the same right to act for the firm in partnership transactions in the absence of stipulations to the contrary. Therefore, such a partner may be liable for firm obligations as are other general partners.

The terms junior partner and senior partner, while frequently used in law firms and other professional partnerships, have no special legal significance other than that which may be given to the terms in the specific partnership agreement. This occurs in some states where it is permissible for the partners, by written agreement, to establish the rights, powers, and duties of the junior partners as distinguished from the senior partners. Also, the agreement may provide for the varying rights and duties of non-partner employees, such as associates, non-partner members, and others.

Where a written agreement between the so-called junior partner and the firm does not give the junior partner the right of part ownership of the business (an indispensible requirement under the Uniform Act) he has been held by some courts not to be a partner. But there have also been some decisions to the effect that a junior partner, who has little or no voice in the management of the firm, may be liable for the losses of the partnership as any other partner. This question will, of course, depend primarily upon the particular facts and cir-

cumstances of each case. The written agreement should plainly
state the status and responsibilities of each partner to avoid
confusion and uncertainty.

Partnership as a Separate Entity

The adoption of the Uniform Partnership Act did not, as
might have been expected, resolve the question as to the true
nature of a partnership. An attempt was made in the early
drafts of the act to define a partnership as "a legal person
formed by the association of two or more individuals for the
purpose of carrying on a business with a view to profit." The
final draft of the act left the entity question unanswered. And
the question has not yet been fully resolved.

Therefore, the various definitions of partnership do not
clearly answer the question whether a partnership is a legal
entity. Legal entity means a being or artificial person recognized by law as having rights, powers, and duties distinct from
the individual persons making up such entity. While a corporation is recognized as a separate, legal entity for most purposes,
there has been a considerable dispute as to whether a partnership is a legal entity or merely an aggregate of persons
acting together.

There are two opposing theories on the nature of a partnership. One theory, sometimes called the "Entity Theory,"
is that a partnership is a distinct and separate entity from the
partners, just as a corporation is a distinct and separate entity from the stockholders. The other, called the "Aggregate
Theory," is that partners are co-owners of the firm and the
firm property. Under the Entity Theory, a partner can deal
with his firm just as if it were another entity. The Aggregate
Theory views dealings between partner and partnership as
a combination of a deal between one partner and his other partners and another deal with himself. Consequently, a particular
transaction may result in different outcomes from a legal and
tax viewpoint. The Entity Theory cannot be reconciled with
the basic principle of partnership law that each partner is liable
and responsible for partnership debts and obligations.

A review of the Uniform Act indicates that many of its rules are based on the Entity Theory. The act provided for the ownership and conveyance of property in the firm's name, the continuity of the partnership notwithstanding the assignment of a partner's interest, the priority of partnership creditors in reference to partnership assets, and the fiduciary duty of a partner to the firm. The act does apply the Aggregate Theory in establishing joint and several liability for partners.

Statutes may, of course, specifically treat partnerships as entities. The Federal Bankruptcy Act treats a partnership as a distinct legal entity, as does the Uniform Commercial Code. One of the important points in the area of partnership taxation is that the partnership, as such, is not a taxable entity. It is merely a form of doing business by two or more persons who are liable for any tax in their individual capacities. Each partner picks up his or her share of the partnership's income or loss on his or her income tax returns.

The result is that the courts frequently hold that, in some respects and for some purposes, a partnership may be regarded as a legal entity. It is equally well settled that it is not such an entity as is a natural person or a corporation, and that its status as an independent entity is limited and incomplete. The courts point out that a partnership is an entity only for certain limited purposes, such as for facilitating transfers of property, marshalling assets, and protecting the business operations against the impact of personal involvement of the partners, or for other purposes.

Limited Partnership

Most states have special statutes which authorize the formation of limited partnerships. These permit individuals, upon compliance with the statutory requirements, to contribute specified sums to the capital of a partnership firm, and then limit their liability to the amount of their capital contribution. This is somewhat like the relationship of a stockholder to a corporation.

The general purpose of the Uniform Limited Partnership Act, which has been adopted in almost all states, is to allow a form of business enterprise, other than a corporation, in which persons can invest their money without becoming liable as general partners for all debts of the partnership.

According to the Uniform Limited Partnership Act a limited partnership is formed by two or more persons under that act, having as members one or more general partners and one or more limited partners. The act specifically declares that limited partners, basically interested in investing, are not bound by the obligations of participating in the partnership. The general partner's rights, powers, and obligations are similar to those of partners in a general partnership.

The general partner may become individually liable for all debts of the firm. He or she is accountable to other partners as a fiduciary. The act restricts his or her authority in a number of ways. It also provides that he or she may be a general partner and a limited partner in the same partnership at the same time. In this situation this person has all the rights, powers, limitations, and liabilities of a general partner.

The Uniform Limited Partnership Act provides that a partnership may carry on any business which a partnership without limited partners may carry on, except those specified in the act. Generally, a limited partnership may not engage in the banking or insurance businesses. Check your local statutes for specific business information.

Partnerships Compared with Other Entities

A partnership is clearly distinguishable from a corporation. A corporation is an artificial person or entity created by law as the representative of those persons who contribute to, or become holders of, shares in the property entrusted to it for a common purpose. A corporation is a separate entity distinct from its individual members or stockholders, who, as natural persons, are merged in the corporate identity. The stockholders are generally not personally liable for any of the obligations of the corporation. On the other hand, each partner is

individually liable for the debts and obligations of a partnership and for the acts of the other partners, so far as the acts
are within the scope or apparent scope of their authority as
partners.

A corporation can act only through a direct vote of the
shareholders or by officers or agents authorized for the purpose, and the shareholders of the corporation, as such, cannot bind the corporation. But in a partnership each member
binds as a principal.

Although a corporation can, in effect, be owned by one
shareholder, a single individual cannot be the owner of a partnership. The law does not permit a partnership to do business
under the guise of a corporation. One of the essential elements
of a partnership is joint ownership.

In a sole proprietorship, discussed in more detail in Part
III, the individual person is wholly and personally liable for
all of his or her debts without regard to whether they may
be incurred for personal or business reasons. He or she is a
single, legal entity who cannot separate business debts or
assets from those incurred personally. The sole proprietor is
also in absolute and complete charge of the management and
control of the business.

A joint venture is an association of two or more persons to
carry out a single business for profit which is usually, but not
necessarily, limited to a single transaction. Liability is limited
only by the fact that it is usually a single transaction and by
the duration which is usually limited to a short period of time.
The joint venture is governed by the same basic principles
of law as are partnerships.

It is sometimes difficult to distinguish cases between joint
ventures and partnerships. The legal relationships of the parties to a joint venture and the nature of their associations are
quite similar and closely akin to a partnership. Despite the
similarities, there are important distinctions between the two,
the most important being the single nature of joint venture,
the fact that loss sharing is not essential, and the eligibility
of corporations for membership.

A partnership is also to be distinguished from a grubstake
arrangement, a very loose, informal compact whereby one par-

ty undertakes to supply finances and equipment which another party uses in discovering and locating mineral claims, after which the two parties share in any claims located as a result of such operations.

A partnership is different from all types of joint ownership of real and personal property. Although joint ownership of property is an essential element of a partnership, joint ownership, in and of itself, is not sufficient to constitute a legal partnership. Partnership property has many of the characteristics of an estate in common and of joint tenancy or cotenancy. However, the interest of the partners in the firm property, under the Uniform Partnership Act, is called tenancy in partnership. A partnership arises out of a contract between the parties, whereas a joint ownership in property may be created by operation of law.

Since by definition a partnership must carry on a business for profit, it is generally recognized that a non-profit organization is different. Among these types of organizations not considered partnerships are fraternal orders, beneficial societies, patriotic organizations, civic societies, political committees or parties, religious organizations or societies, and sport or recreation associations.

Other associations which do not earn profits, although they may be formed for the purpose of achieving economic benefits for their members, would not qualify as legal partnerships. Included in this category are trade and professional associations and labor unions. However, the members of a voluntary association of individuals or of an unincorporated company organized for profit may be considered partners in their relationship to third persons.

A partnership association is a unique business organization which closely resembles the corporation. Members enjoy limited liability and the association is a separate entity for most purposes. The members have the right to control membership in the association. Interests in the association can be transferred, but the new owner may not participate in the management of the business unless he is elected to membership. These organizations are permitted in only a few states, and you should carefully check the particular statute before utilizing

it. The main purpose is to enable persons desiring to combine
their capital in any business enterprise to do so without in-
curring the general liability of partners or the risk of having
the business taken out of the control of those in whom it was
placed without the original members' consent.

A joint stock company is an association of individuals
possessing a common capital divided into shares that represent the interests owned by the members. The shares are
transferable without the consent of the other members and
there is no dissolution upon the death, bankruptcy, or insanity of a member. It is like a corporation in that it has a separate
name, but it is like a partnership in that there is unlimited
liability of members.

A trust, in this sense, is an agreement, almost invariably
in writing, in which one person or persons, called settlor or
donor, conveys assets or property to another person or persons, called trustee, for the use and benefit of another person
or persons, called beneficiary. The property is held, administered, and maintained in accordance with the instruction
by the settlor contained in the written agreement.

A partnership is distinguishable from a trust in that a partnership involves joint ownership while a trust involves representative ownership. A trustee has a fiduciary duty to the
beneficiary, just as a partner has to another partner; however,
the converse is not true. A beneficiary has no duty or obligation to the trustee. Moreover, the beneficiary of a trust does
not usually become involved in the management or operation
of the trust as do partners. In a trust situation, the trustee
is not ordinarily responsible for any losses or profits from the
administration of the trust. although partnerships and trusts
have similarities, it is easy to specify in a written document
just what arrangements the parties intend.

Selection of Your Business Organization

The factors typically discussed and considered in the process of selecting a business organization include:
- simplicity
- organizational flexibility
- financing
- continuity
- transferability of interests
- goodwill
- estate liquidity
- splitting of income among family members
- expenses involved in organization
- personal liability exposure
- centralization of management and control and
- tax factors

You will need to make an analysis of your situation, consider the relative importance and significance of the various factors involved, and make a selection which will comply with most of your needs. Generally, the exposure to personal liability is one of the negative factors in a partnership.

Preparation of Your Own Partnership Agreement

A partnership, as a type of voluntary association, must find its basis in an expressed or implied agreement between the partners. The agreement, like most other contracts, need not be in writing to be legally binding. But you are strongly advised to insist upon a written agreement. There is always the problem of proving the existence of a partnership and, if there is no written agreement, this can be troublesome. Moreover, if the agreement was not in writing, when disputes arise as to its terms and conditions, usually after the parties have some disagreement, the question of what was intended in the beginning may never be resolved satisfactorily. If, after full discussions, a carefully drafted agreement is signed, there can be far less doubt about the intent and understanding of the parties.

Also, keep in mind that there are some situations in which an agreement must be in writing and signed by the parties to be legally valid. Those are the situations listed under your state statute of frauds. Usually included within this statute are real estate transactions, agreements that by their terms are not to be performed within one year after the making thereof, and agreements to answer for the debt, default, or miscarriage of another. A word to the wise: when in doubt, put it in writing.

There may be major tax factors that suggest having a written agreement. The Uniform Act provides that a partnership is subject to the extensive and detailed regulations of your state statutes unless you have a written agreement to the contrary. It is extremely important for you to create a written document that clearly reflects the rights and obligations that the parties intend to assume in their association with you. The topics listed in this book which you should consider in preparing a partnership agreement are taken from the typical transactions of the business community, and are selected with a view of avoiding disputes and disagreements. To the extent that you can avoid one single lawsuit, you will have saved your money, time, frustration, and embarrassment.

The Partnership Agreement

A contract, express or implied is essential to the formation of a partnership. The words *contract* and *agreement,* as used herein, are synonymous. A contract is a promise, or set of promises, for the breach of which the law gives a remedy, or for the performance of which the law recognizes a duty. The duties and obligations of partners arising from a partnership agreement are regulated as far as they are covered by the written contract. A written agreement between partners constitutes the measure of the partner's rights and obligations. The written agreement may include practically any provision you desire so long as it is lawful. Where the written agreement does not cover situations or questions which arise, they are determined under applicable statutory law. If a question is not answered by the provisions of the statutes, it will be controlled by common law rules.

The existence of a partnership may be proven by transactions, conduct, and declarations in situations where there is no written agreement. As in the case of any contract, the consent of the parties is required to make a partnership contract enforceable. You cannot be made a partner by operation of law alone, but only by your voluntary acts. The Uniform Act provides that no person can become a member of a partnership without the consent of all the partners. A third person may charge another with partnership liability even in the absence of the existence of an actual partnership relation if there has been conduct leading the third person to believe there was a partnership. Such liability can be imposed on the alleged partner only upon the basis of his voluntary conduct permitted others to hold him out as partner. This is called *partnership by estoppel.* This rule presents another strong reason for you to insist upon a written agreement to govern any business transaction in which you wish to participate.

Tests or Indicia of Partnerships

In determining whether a partnership exists, the courts will take numerous factors into account. Where parties expressly agree to unite their property and services as joint owners to carry on a business for a profit, and to share the profits and losses in stated proportions, there exists an agreement that clearly creates a partnership. But where the agreement between persons engaged in a business enterprise which is supposed to create a partnership relation is uncertain in its terms, as is often the case, or where the persons have never executed a formal, written expression of their relation, the courts have encountered great difficulty in formulating tests by which to determine the existence or non-existence of a partnership relation. Reports are abundant with cases applying differing tests and indicia of a partnership relation, and differing conclusions have been reached, with the result that the decisions are so conflicting on the subject that it is impossible to reconcile them. These perplexing problems were among the many reasons that prompted the drafting of the Uniform Act, and the reasons for the advice to put your agreements in writing.

The Uniform Act provides certain rules for determining whether a partnership exists. But these rules are not all inclusive. Mainly, they are refinements of previous rules established by the courts. The draftsmen of the act tacitly acknowledged the fact that a partnership is a contractual relationship that may vary in form and substance in an almost infinite variety of ways, by stating in the most general language an assortment of rules to be considered in determining whether a partnership exists.

In the last analysis, there is no arbitrary test for determining the existence of a partnership, and each case must be decided according to its particular facts. Confusion in the interpretation and application of decisions results when the tests are applied indiscriminately without keeping in mind a certain indication of partnership may be of considerable significance in one case and not in another. Generally, the elements considered critical to the existence of a partnership are intention of two or more persons to be partners, sharing of profits and losses, joint ownership and control of the capital assets or property of the group, and joint control and management of the business.

Sharing of Profits

Under the English doctrine from 1600 to 1850, which was followed by the American decisions, persons sharing the profits of a commercial enterprise were liable to creditors as if they were actual partners. These early authorities treated the sharing of the profits as a conclusive test of the existence of a partnership, particularly as to third persons. Some courts also adopted this test in situations in which the rights of the parties, among themselves, were involved. The reason given for this test was that by taking part in the profits, there was taken from the creditors a part of that fund which was a security for the payment of their debts. In the course of time, important exceptions were introduced. Under these exceptions the early rule was not applied where the participant did not receive the profits as "principal or as profits," or where the profits were received as compensation for services rendered or in payment as rent to a landlord, or as a debt or interest on a loan. Ultimately the rule was abolished.

The current view, adopted by most courts, is that the sharing of profits is not, of itself, sufficiently conclusive to show the existence of a partnership relation. Participation in the profits does not necessarily make the recipient a legal partner, especially where there is no intention, joint ownership of the business, or other essentials of a valid partnership. In other words, participation in the profits is only regarded as a circumstance to be considered, among others, in determining whether or not a partnership existed. In order for a partnership to exist, there must be an ownership interest in the profits of the business.

Joint Ownership of Property

Although the profit and loss category is the most significant, it is not in and of itself sufficient to constitute a partnership. The ownership of the assets of a going business is also an important factor in determining whether a partnership exists.

Joint Management and Control of Business

Where one owns an interest in property and shares in the profits and losses, it is almost certain that he or she will exercise some degree of control over the management of the business. This is, again, only one of the factors that the courts examine in deciding on the existence of a partnership. Of course, the final determination is a question of fact and will depend upon the conclusions reached by a judge or jury based upon an evaluation of all of the facts and circumstances involved in a transaction. It is easy to see that a written agreement would eliminate the necessity of going through such a fact finding procedure.

The "Rendering Services" Relationship: Employee or Partner?"

Various factors will determine whether a relationship is one of partnership or of employment. A person rendering services does not become a partner merely because he or she receives a share of the profits of the business, but an agreement to share losses as well as profits is a strong indication of the existence of a partnership. The fact that a party rendering services assumes financial obligations by agreeing to make capital contributions, or by furnishing credit, or by participating in the expenses necessary to produce profits, has been held suggestive of a partnership contract, and conversely, the lack of any obligations of this kind has been held to indicate an employment contract.

The fact that one rendering services for another is possessed, jointly with the other party or parties to the contract, of a property right in lands, chattels, moneys, or assets which are used to produce the profits, tends to indicate a partnership relation, and conversely, the lack of such property right suggests an employment contract. Where a party rendering services has rights of managing and determining the policies of the enterprise equal with those of the other party or parties to the contract, or permits the use of his or her name in the business operation, it tends to indicate a partnership.

The Uniform Act defines a partnership and states the rules for determining the existence of a partnership as follows:

Section 6. Partnership Defined
- A partnership is an association of two or more persons to carry on as co-owners a business for profit.
- But an association formed under any other statute of this state, or any statute adopted by authority, other than the authority of this state, is not a partnership under this act unless such association would have been a partnership in this state prior to the adoption of this act; but this act shall apply to limited partnerships except in so far as the statutes relating to such partnerships are inconsistent herewith.

Section 7. Rules for Determining the Existence of a Partnership.
In determining whether a partnership exists, these rules shall apply:
- Except as provided by Section 16, persons who are not partners as to each other are not partners as to third persons.
- Joint tenancy, tenancy in common, tenancy by the entireties, joint property, common property, or part ownership does not of itself establish a partnership, whether such co-owners do or do not share any profits made by the use of the property.
- The sharing of gross returns does not of itself establish a partnership, whether or not the persons sharing them have a joint or common right or interest in any property from which the returns are derived.

- The receipt by a person of a share of the profits of a business is prima-facie evidence that he is a partner in the business, but no such inference shall be drawn if such profits were received in payment:

  As a debt by installments or otherwise;

  As wages of an employee or rent to a landlord;

  As an annuity to a widow or representative of a deceased partner;

  As interest on a loan, though the amount of payment vary with the profits of the business;

  As the consideration for the sale of a goodwill of a business or other property by installments or otherwise.

Section 8. Partnership Property

- All property originally brought into the partnership stock or subsequently acquired by purchase or otherwise, on account of the partnership, is partnership property.
- Unless the contrary intention appears, property acquired with partnership funds is partnership property.
- Any estate in real property may be acquired in the partnership name. Title so acquired can be conveyed only in the partnership name.
- A conveyance to a partnership in the partnership name, though without words of inheritance, passes the entire estate of the grantor unless a contrary intent appears.

Partners as to Third Persons—Estoppel

At common law, that is, prior to the adoption of the Uniform Act, the courts had frequently stated that persons who were not partners as to each other, but who held themselves out as partners, were partners as to third persons, and were subject to the liabilities of partners. Some cases which were decided after the adoption of the Uniform Act still base the liability of individuals on the fact that they are partners as to third persons. This liability is based on the doctrine of estoppel, and on the policy of the law seeking to prevent frauds on those who lend their money on the apparent credit of those who are held out as partners. But in view of the specific provisions of the Uniform Act, the courts generally recognize that persons who are not partners, as among themselves, are not partners as to third persons, unless the principle of estoppel is applicable. The modern rule is that, while technically there is no such status as partners as to third persons, in some instances persons may, under the application of the doctrine of estoppel, become liable as if they were partners.

The liability as a partner of a person who holds himself or herself out as a partner, or permits others to do so, is predicated on the doctrine of equitable estoppel. This is the common law rule which is codified in the Uniform Code. While the existence of a partnership may be proved by any competent evidence, the best evidence consists of the agreement or contract between the parties.

The provision in the Uniform Act relating to partnership by estoppel is as follows:

Section 16. Partnership by Estoppel

• When a person, by words spoken or written or by conduct, represents himself, or consents to another representing him to any one, as a partner in an existing partnership or with one or more persons not actually partners, he is liable to any such person to whom such representation has been made, who has, on the faith of such representation, given credit to the actual or apparent partnership, and if he has made such representation or consented to its being made in a public manner he is liable to such person, whether the representation has or has not been made or communicated to such person so giving credit by or with the knowledge of the apparent partner making the representation or consenting to its being made.

> *When a partnership liability results, he is liable as though he were an actual member of the partnership.*

> *When no partnership liability results, he is liable jointly with the other persons, if any, so consenting to the contract or representation as to incur liability, otherwise separately.*

• When a person has been thus represented to be a partner in an existing partnership, or with one or more persons not actual partners, he is an agent of the persons consenting to such representation to bind them to the same extent and in the same manner as though he were a partner in fact, with respect to persons who rely upon the representation. Where all the members of the existing partnership consent to the representation, a partnership act or obligation results; but in all other cases it is the joint act or obligation of the person acting and the person consenting to the representation.

Preparing Your Contract

You can benefit from all of the past disputes and mistakes which have occurred between partners if you study the rules and understand and appreciate the problems which may arise provided, of course, you prepare a written agreement for your business transactions *before* they get under way.

In order to give you a full and complete understanding of the requirements for a written partnership agreement, each and every part of a full, complete, comprehensive, and legally valid partnership agreement is listed and discussed below. Alternative, additional, and supplemental provisions and suggestions are also provided. In addition, several sample partnership agreements will be given. You will be able to select one of the simple agreements, or parts of several of them, and by adding, deleting, and amending as appropriate, draft your own partnership agreement which has all of the items necessary for a final, formal business document. However, it is strongly recommended that you do not attempt to prepare your partnership agreement until you have carefully read and studied the entire text of this section.

Checklist of Facts and Information You Should Consider in Preparing Your Partnership Agreement

Before you start any work on your partnership agreement, you should carefully study the checklist which follows, and make provisions for all items which may arise in connection with your business arrangements. By doing this you will be certain to avoid or resolve disputes, disagreements, and misunderstandings that typically arise in the conduct of business.

- In what name will the partnership business be conducted?
- What are the names and addresses of the partners?
- What type of business is to be conducted?
- Where is the business to be located?
- Term of existence:
  What date is the business to be started?
  How long is the business to continue?
- Capital of the partnership:
  How much capital is to be invested by each partner?
  How much is to be invested in cash?
  How much is to be invested in property other than cash?
  When is property or cash to be paid into partnership?
  What arrangements are to be made for additional capital?
- How are profits and losses to be divided between the partners?
- What salaries are partners to receive?
- Are partners to be permitted drawing accounts?
- Are partners to receive interest on capital investment?
- Duties of partners:
  Are partners to devote their time exclusively to the business?
  What specific functions will each partner perform?
  What are the rights of each partner in management of the partnership business?
- Disposal of partnership interest:
  Will partner be permitted to sell his or her interest?
  Should partner be prohibited from selling his or her interest?
- Banking of funds:
  What is the name of bank?
  Who is to sign checks?
- Books of account:
  Where are the books to be kept?
  What provisions are to be made for auditing by accountants?
- Termination or dissolution:
  How shall the partnership be terminated?
  Does either partner have the right to continue business upon termination?

> *What are the rights of partners to return of capital contributions?*
> *What procedure shall be used to liquidate the business?*

- Death of partners:
> *What are the rights of the survivors?*
> *What is the purchase price of decedents' interest or how shall it be determined?*
> *What provision is to be made to continue the business?*
> *What provision is to be made to liquidate the business?*

- Disability of partners:
> *What are the rights of a partner who has been disabled or is unable to perform his or her duties as partner upon disability?*
> *What are the rights of partners to purchase a disabled partner's share in the partnership?*

- Are provisions to be made for admitting additional partners?

- Are provisions to be made for arbitration of controversies?

- Are provisions to be made for retirement of partners?

- Are provisions to be made to expel a partner whose misconduct, inattention to business, or other action seriously injures the business?

- Use of partnership name:
> *May partnership name be continued upon the death of partner?*
> *May partnership name be continued upon the retirement of partner?*
> *May partnership name be continued upon sale of business?*

- How is title to partnership assets to be taken?

- Shall provision be made not to divulge trade secrets?

- Shall provision be made for retiring partners not to compete in business?

- Shall provision be made that no partner shall become maker, endorser, or surety of any obligation without consent?

- What restrictions shall be made on outside activities of partners?
- Are partners to be bonded?
- Are provisions to be made for goodwill of business?
- Are provisions to be made for life insurance?
- Are partners to be limited in any manner as to their power or authority to act as agent of the partnership?
- Are provisions to be made to amend this partnership agreement?

When you have determined the answers to these questions, you will be able to select the appropriate parts for your partnership agreement from the forms that follow. You will begin your agreement with introductory clauses.

Sample Partnership Agreement Forms

Introductory Clauses

Most written agreements begin with the date, identification of the parties, statement of the place of residence of each, and a statement of the purpose and intention of the written document. Although these are not absolutely essential to the validity of a contract, they are important, helpful, and should appear at some place in the document. There are many different forms that are frequently used, and the following are the most popular samples. Begin your agreement with one of these statements.

Sample 1:

This agreement of partnership made and entered into this _____ day of _____, 19_____, by and between _____, _____, and _____,   all of the City of _____, County of _____, State of _____, witness and agree as follows:

Sample 2:

It is hereby understood and agreed between _____, party of the first part, and _____, party of the second part, that _____.

Sample 3:

This Partnership Agreement entered into on _____, between _____, of _____, and _____, of _____, Witnesseth:

Name of Partnership or Business

Sample 1:
The firm name of the said partnership shall be _____
_____ .

Sample 2:
The business of the said partnership shall be carried on under the firm name of _____.

Duration

Term

Sample 1:
This partnership shall continue for the term of _____ years from the date of this agreement.

Sample 2:
This partnership shall continue until the death of the parties, unless previously terminated, but either party may terminate it at will upon giving _____ days' notice to the other partners.

Sample 3:
The said _____, _____, _____, and _____, and the survivors of them, will become and remain partners in the business of _____ from the _____ day of _____, 19_____, during the term of _____ years, if they or any two of them shall so long live, under the firm name of _____ _____, subject, nevertheless, to termination as hereinafter provided.

After Retirement or Death of Partner

Sample 1:
Any partner may retire from the partnership on or at any time after the _____ day of _____, 19_____, on giving not less than _____ months' previous written notice to the others of his intention to do so, and at the expiration of such notice, the partnership shall terminate so far as regards the partner giving or leaving such notice, but not as between the remaining partners.

Sample 2:
The death of any partner shall not dissolve the partnership between the remaining partners.

Sample 3:
Should any partner die during the term of this agreement, the firm shall not be dissolved thereupon, but the business shall be continued by the survivors until the expiration of the term, the estate of the deceased partner to bear the same share in profits and losses as would have been received and borne by the deceased partner, had he lived.

Place of Business

Sample 1:
The partnership business and operations shall be carried on at _____, or at such places as the partners shall from time to time determine.

Sample 2:
The offices of said firm shall be situated at _____
_____ .

Purpose

Sample 1:
This partnership shall be for the purpose of buying, selling, and dealing in _____ .

Sample 2:
The object of this partnership shall be to engage generally in the business of _____, and its allied arts and trades, and of buying, selling, and generally dealing in all goods, merchandise, and supplies incidental thereto.

Sample 3:
This partnership is for the purpose of buying, developing, and selling a certain tract of land described as follows: _____
_____ ,
and for no other purpose.

Capital

General Forms
Sample 1:
   The capital of the partnership shall be_____
dollars, and each partner shall contribute equally thereto (or in the
shares or proportions following, namely _____) or
in such shares as may from time to time be agreed upon in writing.

Sample 2:
   Each partner shall leave in the business each year as an addition
to the partnership capital an amount equal to _____
of the profits distributable to him at the time of each annual
accounting.

Sample 3:
   The stock in trade and plant now owned by the said _____
shall be taken to be of the value of_____
dollars, and shall become the partnership property of such valuation, and shall be credited to the said _____ on
account of the capital which he is to contribute.

One Partner Furnishing Capital
   The said _____ shall at once bring into the business
the sum of _____ dollars as capital, which shall
be employed in the said business, and for the benefit of the partnership, during the partnership term, without any allowance of interest
for its use, and shall, from time to time, at the request of the said
_____, advance and bring into the said business
such further sums of money (not exceeding the sum of_____
dollars in any one year, nor exceeding, together with the said sum
of _____ dollars, the total sum of   _____
dollars) as shall, in the opinion of the said _____,
be required for carrying on the said business, and shall be allowed
interest on such further advances at the rate of _____ percent per
annum out of the profits of the said business, before any division
of such profits.

One Partner Without Capital

The said_____shall furnish the sum of_____dollars as capital to carry on the business. The said _____ shall devote his entire time, services, and skill to the management of the business and shall not be required to contribute to the capital stock of the partnership, and shall share equally in profits and losses (including depreciation in capital) with the other partners.

Increase of Capital

If, at any time hereafter, further capital shall be required for carrying on the business, and a majority of the partners shall determine to increase the capital, the additional capital shall be advanced by the partners in equal shares (or in such proportions as they have respectively contributed to the original capital of the firm).

Additional Capital

If any partner shall, with the other partners' consent, bring in additional capital, or leave any part of his profits in the business, the same shall be considered a debt due to him from the partnership, and shall bear interest at the rate of _____ percent per annum, and shall not be drawn out except upon giving _____ calendar months' written notice; and the partner who has brought in additional capital or left in part of his profits shall be bound to draw out the same on a like notice given to him by the other partners, and at the expiration of such notice interest shall cease to be payable thereon.

Dormant Partner

Said _____ shall contribute the sum of _____ dollars to the firm, as his share of the capital thereof, but shall have no active part in the management of the business of the firm, nor shall his name be used in the firm name, nor in any advertising of the firm, but shall be entitled to _____ percent of the profits, if any, of the firm, and shall bear _____ percent of the losses, if any, of the firm.

Advances

Any partner may from time to time, with the consent of the others, advance any sums of money to the firm by way of loan, and every such advance shall bear interest at the rate of _____ percent per annum, from the time of making the advance until repayment thereof, and may be withdrawn at any time on _____ months' notice.

Expenses

All rent, expenses for repairs or improvements, all taxes, premiums of insurance, salaries and wages, and any and all other reasonable and necessary expenses, losses and damages which may be incurred in carrying on the partnership business (and the interest on the capital, payable to the respective partners), shall be paid out of the receipts and earnings of the said business, and in case such receipts and earnings are insufficient to pay such charges, the said partners shall contribute thereto in the shares or proportions in which they are entitled to the profits of the business.

Profits, Compensation, and Drawing Accounts

Division of Profits and Losses

Sample 1:

Each partner herein shall share in all profits or losses of the business in the same proportion as his share in the capital of the firm bears to the total capital of the firm.

Sample 2:

The profits and losses shall belong to, and be borne by, _____ and _____ in equal shares.

Guaranty of Profits

In case the share of _____ in the net profits shall in any year be less than _____ dollars, such share shall in every such year be made up to_____dollars by the other partners, by contributions in proportion to the shares in which they are entitled to the net profits.

Drawing Accounts

Each partner shall be at liberty, from time to time, to draw out of the business any sum or sums of money, not exceeding the sum of_____dollars per month, for his own use; all such sums, at the time of drawing the same, to be entered in the cashbook, and to be duly accounted for on every settlement of accounts and divisions of the profits of the business.

Salary

____, the managing partner, shall receive as compensation during the term of this agreement a salary of $_____ per month in addition to his share of the profits, and the salary shall be considered as an expense of the firm.

Regular Meetings

On Friday of each week, at 9:00 a.m., there shall be a meeting of the partners, at the office of the firm, for the purpose of going over expense accounts for the preceding week, and for the further purpose of discussing and acting upon the general conduct of the business of the partnership. For any matters within the scope of the business, and within this or supplemental contracts, a majority of the partners present at any such meeting shall prevail. Any change of the scope or nature of the business, however, shall not be made except by and with the knowledge and consent of all of the partners.

Books and Accounts

Keeping Accounts

Proper books of accounts shall be kept at the office of the firm, in which shall be entered all the dealings and transactions of the partnership. The books shall at all times be open to the inspection of all or any of the partners, and be kept constantly posted and current.

Taking Accounts

The partners, once in each year, namely, on the _____ day of _____ in each and every year, or more often if necessary, shall make and render, each to the other, full and correct inventories and accounts of all profits and increase by them or either of them made, and of all losses by them or either of them sustained; and also of all payments, receipts, disbursements, and all other things by them made, received, disbursed, acted, done, or suffered in the partnership and business; and upon the rendering of every such account shall clear, adjust, pay, and deliver, each to the other, their just share of the profits so made as aforesaid.

Restrictions on Authority of Partners

Limits upon Contracts by One Partner

Neither partner, without the previous consent in writing of the others, shall buy or sell or enter into any contract for the purchase or sale of any goods or other articles amounting to the value of _____ dollars or more.

Negotiable Paper

All checks, notes, and other writings pledging the credit or affecting the property of the partnership, shall be signed by _____ or _____, and not otherwise.

Bonds and Securities

Whenever there shall be occasion to give any bond, note, bill, or other security for the payment of any money on account of the partnership, the same shall be respectively signed and executed by all the partners.

Suretyship

No partner shall, without the others' previous written consent, enter into any bond, or become bail, surety, or security, for any person.

Extending Credit

No partner shall lend any money, or give credit to, or have dealings on behalf of the partnership with, any person, partnership, or corporation whom the other partners or partner shall have forbidden him to trust or deal with; and if he shall act contrary to this provision, he shall repay to the partnership any loss which may have been incurred thereby.

Pledging Credit

No partner shall pledge the credit of the firm or use any money, goods, or effects of the partnership except in the ordinary course of business, and upon the account or for the benefit of the partnership.

Release of Debts

No partner shall, without consent of the others, compound, release, or discharge any debt which shall be due or owing to the partnership, without receiving the full amount thereof.

Hiring Employees

No partner shall hire or dismiss, unless in case of gross misconduct, any clerk or any other person in the employment of the partnership, without the other partners' consent.

Retirement of Partner

Withdrawal of Partner

Any partner may retire at any time from the partnership, upon giving written notice of his intention to do so, to the other partners personally, and the partnership shall determine as to him _____ months after the date of said notice; but the other partners may purchase his interest at a fair valuation and carry on the business.

Retiring Partner Not to Compete

In the event of any of the said partners retiring as aforesaid, he shall not, during the remainder of the term of the said partnership, carry on or engage or be interested, directly or indirectly, in any other business competing or interfering with the business of the firm, subject, however, to any applicable statute to the contrary.

Retiring Partner to Be Indemnified

In case any partner shall at any time withdraw from the partnership, and shall sell his interest therein to the remaining partners, or, in case of dissolution, when a part of said partners shall purchase the interest of the other partners, then such purchasing partners shall give good and sufficient bond to such withdrawing partner, to the reasonable satisfaction of such withdrawing partner, in an amount equal to the amount of the debts of the firm, conditioned on the payment in full of all outstanding debts of said firm, when due, and for the savings of such withdrawing partner, of any loss which might occur to such withdrawing partner, by reason of the nonpayment of such debts as herein provided.

Dissolution

Dissolution in Case of Loss

In case the net assets of the partnership shall at any time fall below the sum of _____ dollars, then any member thereof, in spite of the fact that the partnership has not expired by lapse of time, may withdraw from the firm, and commence an action for the dissolution of the firm.

Winding up Business

Upon dissolution of the partnership, a full and general account of the firm assets, liabilities, and transactions shall be taken, and the assets and property of the firm shall, as soon as practicable, be sold, the debts due the partnership collected, the proceeds to be applied, first, in the discharge of the firm liabilities and the expenses of liquidating the same; and next, in payment to each partner or his representatives of any unpaid interest or profits belonging to him, and of his share of the capital; and the surplus, if any, shall be divided between the partners or their representatives in the shares in which they contributed the firm capital; and the partners or their representatives shall execute all requisite or proper instruments for facilitating the collection and division of the partnership property and for their mutual indemnity and release.

Goodwill

On the death or retirement of any partner no allowance (or an allowance) shall be made to him or his representatives in respect of the value of the goodwill of the said business.

Division of Property

At the expiration of this agreement the parties herein shall each give all possible aid to arrive at a just and true account of all the assets and liabilities. The assets, including the goodwill of said business, shall first be offered for sale to the partners herein, and the partner offering the most for the same shall be allowed to purchase the same. In case there is no partner who desires to purchase the assets, then the assets shall be sold to whomever shall pay the most therefor. In either event, all liabilities shall be paid for out of the proceeds of such sale. The net amount secured by such sale shall be divided among the parties, in proportion to their interest in the firm, at such time of dissolution.

Deceased Partner's Interest

The executors or administrators of any partner who shall die during the partnership, or any person or persons to whom he may, by will, bequeath his share in the partnership, shall be entitled to his share in the firm, capital stock, property, and effects, and may either continue as partner or partners in the business in respect and to the extent of his share and interest of such deceased partner, or may sell the same in the manner hereinabove provided with respect to a sale by any living partner of his share and interest.

Close of Contract

In witness whereof, we hereunto set out hands, this _____ day of _____, 19____, at _____, _____.

_____   _____
(Witnesses, if any)   (Signatures)

Sample Partnership Agreements

The forms that follow contain the essentials for a clear, understandable agreement that you can easily add to or delete from to prepare a written agreement which expresses the understanding and intent of your situation.

You will note that the forms below include several complete partnership agreements and several alternative, additional, or supplemental provisions. In most situations, one of the form agreements, with minor changes, deletions, or additions, will suffice for completion of a proper agreement. In other situations, depending upon the particular facts and circumstances, and depending upon the answers to the check list questions, you can formulate a proper agreement by use of the appropriate provision in the list of forms. In the event you need to cover some special or unusual subject, simply add other paragraphs to spell out clearly the intent and agreement of the parties.

You should not have any of the provisions in the agreement which are, or may be construed as, contradictory, inconsistent, or confusing. Each provision should be discussed in detail by all partners before the agreement is executed. Having done this, you will have accomplished nearly everything any reasonable person could do to assure a smooth, successful, and rewarding business career.

FORM 19: General Partnership Agreement— Two Partners

This agreement made this _____ day of _____, 19___, between _____ and _____, both of the City of _____, County of _____, State of _____, witness and agree as follows:

1. The parties do hereby agree to form a partnership under the name of _____ for the purpose of conducting a _____ business.

2. The place at which the partnership is to conduct its business is _____.

3. The partnership shall continue until dissolved by mutual agreement.

4. The capital of the partnership shall be contributed equally in cash by the partners.

5. The net profits of the partnership shall be divided equally between the partners, and the net losses shall be borne equally by them.

6. Neither partner shall receive any salary for services rendered to the partnership.

7. Each of the partners shall be permitted such drawing accounts as may be agreed upon between them.

8. Both partners are to devote their entire time and attention to the business. The partners shall have equal rights in the management of the partnership business.

9. The partnership books shall be kept at the place of business and shall be at all times open to inspection by either partner.

10. All funds of the partnership shall be deposited in its name in _____ Bank, and all withdrawals therefrom are to be made upon checks signed by either partner.

11. Either partner may retire from the partnership at the expiration of any fiscal year by giving to the other partner _____ days' notice of his intention to do so. The remaining partner shall have the right either to purchase the retiring partner's interest or to terminate the partnership and liquidate the business. In the event the remaining partner elects to purchase the remaining interest of the retiring partner, the purchase price shall be equal to the book value of the retiring partner's interest in the partnership business as reflected in the partnership books. The purchase price shall be paid by an initial cash payment of $_____, and the balance in _____ installments over a period of _____ years, and shall bear interest on the unpaid balance at the rate of _____ percent per annum.

12. Upon the death of either partner the surviving partner shall have the right either to purchase the interest of the decedent in the partnership or to terminate and liquidate the partnership business. If the surviving partner elects to purchase the decedent's interest, the terms and conditions shall be the same as set forth in the preceding paragraph. If the surviving partner does not elect to purchase the interest of the decedent in the partnership, he shall proceed with reasonable promptness to liquidate the business of the partnership.

IN WITNESS WHEREOF, the parties have signed this Agreement.

_____   _____
(Witnesses, if any)   (Signatures)

# FORM 20: Partnership Agreement— Several Partners—Equal Contributions

This Agreement made this _____ day of _____, 19___, between _____, _____, _____, and _____, all of the City of_____, County of _____,State of _____, witness and agree as follows:

1. Name: The firm name of the partnership shall be____.
2. Purpose: The purpose of the partnership shall be____.
3. Office: The offices of the firm shall be located at ____.
4. Commencement: The partnership shall commence____.
5. Duration: The partnership shall continue until it is dissolved or liquidated.
6. Capital: The capital of the partnership shall be contributed in equal amounts by each partner.
7. Capital Account: An individual capital account shall be maintained for each partner.
8. Withdrawal: No partner shall withdraw any of his capital without the consent of all partners.
9. Capital Gains and Losses: Capital gains and losses shall be shared equally among the partners.
10. Loans by Partners: Interest at the rate of _____ percent per annum shall be allowed on all loans made to the partnership and on all funds left with the firm which the partner would otherwise be entitled to withdraw.
11. Time Devoted to Business: Each partner shall devote his entire time, attention, and ability to partnership affairs
12. Vacations: Each partner shall be entitled to such vacations with salary as may be agreed on.
13. Sickness: When a partner is unable to devote his full time to partnership affairs for reasons of health or otherwise, he shall be entitled to receive such monthly salary and such share of profits as the partners shall determine by vote of the majority in interest.
14. Management: Each partner shall have equal voice in the conduct of the affairs of the business and all decisions shall be by vote of the majority. _____ shall act as General Manager to administer the general affairs of the partnership and to carry out and put into effect the general policies and specific instructions of the majority of the partners.

15. Bank Accounts: The partnership shall maintain checking or other accounts in such bank or banks as the partners shall agree upon. Withdrawal shall be on the signature of _____ and co-signed by _____.

16. Records: All books, records, and accounts of the partnership shall be maintained at the office of the partnership and shall be open to inspection at all times by all partners. For the purpose of partnership accounting and for income tax reporting, the partnership fiscal year shall end on the _____ day of _____ each year. At the end of each month, the books shall be balanced and an operating statement prepared and made available to each partner posting the results of operations during the previous month. The books shall be audited at the end of each fiscal year and statements prepared and supplied to all partners showing the results of operations.

17. Profits and Losses: The partners shall share equally in the profits and losses. As soon as practical after the accounting statements for each fiscal year are approved by all partners, the profits, after salaries of partners, shall be paid to the partners, provided there are funds available in excess of the working capital requirements.

18. Salaries: Until further agreed upon, each partner shall be entitled to a salary of _____ dollars, payable at the end of each month, provided payment of partners' salaries does not impair the capital of the partnership.

19. Limitations on Partners: No partner, without the consent of all other partners, shall borrow money on the partnership name for partnership purposes or utilize collateral owned by the partnership as security for such loans; assign, transfer, pledge, compromise, or release any of the claims or debts due to the partnership except on payment in full; consent to the arbitration of any dispute or controversy of the partnership; transfer firm assets; make, execute, or deliver any assignment for the benefit of creditors; make, execute, or deliver any bond, confession of judgment, guaranty bond, indemnity bond, or surety bond, or any contract to sell, bill of sale, deed, mortgage, or lease relating to any substantial part of the partnership assets or his interest therein; make any purchases in excess of _____ dollars; or engage in any business or occupation without the consent of all other partners.

20. Retirement: Any partner shall have the right to retire from the partnership at the end of any accounting year.

(a) Written notice of intention to retire shall be served upon the other partners at the office of the partnership at least _____ days before the end of the accounting year.

(b) The retirement of any partner shall have no effect upon the continuation of the partnership business.

(c) The remaining partners shall have the right to either purchase the retiring partner's interest or to terminate and liquidate the business.

(d) If the remaining partners elect to purchase the interest of the retiring partner, they shall serve notice in writing of such an election upon the retiring partner at the office of the partnership within _____ days after receipt of his notice of intention to retire.

(e) The purchase price shall be _____ dollars payable in cash and the balance in _____ installments over a period of _____ years and shall be based on the partner's capital interest as set forth in the annual audit.

(f) No allowance shall be made for goodwill, trade name, patents, or other intangible assets, except as those assets have been reflected on the partnership books prior to the annual audit.

(g) If the remaining partners do not elect to purchase the interest of the retiring partner, the remaining partners shall proceed with reasonable promptness to liquidate the business of the partnership.

21. Death: Upon the death of any partner, the surviving partners shall have the right either to purchase the interest of the decedent in the partnership or to terminate and liquidate the partnership business.

(a) If the surviving partners elect to purchase the decedent's interest, they shall serve notice in writing of such election within _____ days after the death of the decedent, upon the executor or administrator of the decedent, or if at the time of such election, no legal representative has been appointed, upon any one of the known legal heirs at the last known address of such heir.

(b) The purchase price and payment thereof shall be the same as set forth in the previous paragraph, except that a physical inventory shall be taken and the partnership books shall be closed and an audit made at the close of business at the end of the current month.

(c) The continuing partners shall have the right to use the firm name of the partnership.

(d) Each of the partners shall have the right to purchase a portion of the decedent's partnership interest in the same proportion which his interest bears to the surviving partner's interest in the partnership.

(e) If the surviving partners do not elect to purchase the entire interest of the decedent, they shall proceed with reasonable promptness to liquidate the business.

(f) The surviving partners and the estates of the deceased partner shall share in the profits and losses of the business during the period of liquidation in the same proportions in which they shared such profits and losses prior to the death of the deceased partner, except that the decedent shall not be liable for losses in excess of the decedent's interest in the partnership at the time of his death.

(g) So long as any surviving partner shall devote his full time to the liquidation of the partnership business, he shall receive a salary at the same rate as he received immediately prior to the decedent's death.

(h) After the payment of partnership debts, the proceeds of liquidation shall be distributed as realized, first in discharge of the undrawn earnings of the partners, including the undrawn earnings of the decedent prior to his death, and the undrawn earnings of his estate during liquidation, then in such manner as to make the capital accounts of the partners proportionate to the capital accounts of the partnership as of the date of its organization, and then proportionately in discharge of the respective capital accounts.

IN WITNESS WHEREOF, the parties have signed and sealed this Agreement this _____ day of _____, 19____.

_____   _____
(Witnesses, if any)   (Signatures)

_____   _____

# FORM 21: Partnership Agreement—Several Partners—Unequal Contributions

This Agreement made this _____ day of _____, 19____, between _____, _____, _____, and _____, all of the City of _____, County of _____, State of _____, witness and agree as follows:

1. The parties do hereby form a partnership under the name of _____, to conduct a business of _____.

2. The principal offices of the partnership shall be located at_____, in the City of_____, State of_____, and at such other place or places as may hereafter be agreed upon by the partners.

3. The partnership shall begin business on the _____ day of _____, 19____, and shall continue for _____ years from said date, or, unless sooner terminated, as herein provided, may be extended for another period or periods by the unanimous consent of the partners above named, evidenced by an endorsement upon this Agreement or by a separate instrument.

4. The capital of the partnership shall consist of_____ dollars of which _____ dollars shall be contributed by _____, above named; _____ dollars by _____, above named; _____ dollars by _____, above named; and _____ dollars by _____, above named.

5. The net profits and net losses of the partnership shall be divided by the partners in proportion to their capital investment.

6. No salaries as such shall be paid to the partners, but each shall be entitled to a drawing account of $ _____ per week, provided said drawing does not impair the capital investment of the partners, and so long as there remains sufficient sums to pay the debts of the partnership.

7. Each partner shall have an equal right in the management of the partnership business and each partner shall devote his entire time to the conduct of said business.

8. All funds of the partnership shall be deposited in its name in the _____ Bank or such other banks as may hereafter be agreed upon between the partners, in such account or accounts as shall be designated by them, and all withdrawals therefrom are to be made by check, signed by any two partners.

9. The partnership shall maintain proper books of accounts of all transactions of the partnership at its place of business, and such books shall be open to inspection at all times to the partners.

10. No partner shall, without the consent of the other partners, compromise or release any debts due the said partnership except upon full payment thereof, or engage in any transaction on behalf of the said partnership of any kind other than those necessary for the transaction of the business of the said partnership, nor make any contract or account of the partnership requiring the expenditure of more than _____ dollars.

11. No partner shall, without the consent of all the other partners, make or endorse, either in the name of the said partnership or individually, any note, or act as an accommodation party, or otherwise become surety for any person. No partner shall, without the consent of all other partners, on behalf of the partnership, borrow or lend money to make, deliver, or accept any commercial paper or execute any mortgage, bond, lease, or other obligation requiring the payment of money, or purchase or contract to purchase or sell any property for or of the partnership other than the type of property bought and sold in the regular course of its business.

12. No partner shall, without the consent of all the other partners, assign, mortgage, or sell his share in the partnership or in its capital, assets, or property thereof, or enter into any agreement as a result of which any person shall become interested with him in the partnership, or do any act detrimental to the business interests of the partnership or which would make it impossible to carry on the ordinary business of the partnership.

13. Each partner shall have the right to retire from the partnership at the end of any fiscal year. Written notice of inten-

tion so to retire shall be served by the partner retiring upon the other partners at the place of business of the partnership at least _____ days before the end of such fiscal year. In case of the retirement of any partner, the remaining partners shall have the right to continue the partnership business or to terminate and liquidate it. If the remaining partners elect to purchase the interest of the retiring partner, they shall serve written notice of such election upon the retiring partner at the office of the partnership within _____ days after receipt of notice of his intention to retire.

14. In the event the remaining partners elect to purchase the interest of the retiring partner in the partnership, the price shall be equal to the book value of the retiring partner's share of the assets of the said partnership. In such event, the firm name shall thereafter be changed so as to remove therefrom the name of the retiring partner. The purchase price shall be paid without interest as follows: _____ percent in cash and the balance by the remaining partners making and delivering to the retiring partner a promissory note which shall be payable in monthly installments over a period of _____ years, bearing no interest. The retiring partner upon receiving the initial cash payment and the said promissory note shall execute and deliver to the remaining partners any and all instruments necessary and proper to transfer and convey to the remaining partners all partnership assets held in his name and his proportionate interest in the partnership assets.

15. If the remaining partners do not purchase the interest of the retiring partner in the partnership, the partners shall procceed with reasonable diligence and prudence to liquidate the business of the partnership. In such liquidation, the partnership assets, including the partnership name and goodwill of the said business, trade names, patents, and other intangible assets, shall be sold for such price as may be reasonably obtained for the same. The partners shall share equally in the profits and losses of the business during the period of liquidation and the proceeds realized from such liquidation shall be divided proportionately between the partners according to their capital investment.

16. Upon the death of any partner during the continuance of the partnership, the surviving partners shall have the right either to purchase the interest of the decedent in the partnership, or to terminate and liquidate the partnership business. If the surviving partners elect to purchase the decedent's interest, they shall serve notice in writing of such election upon the executor, administrator, or other legal representative of the said decedent, personally, within _____ days after the appointment of such legal representative, or if no such legal representative be appointed within _____ days after the death of the said deceased, then upon any one of the known heirs at law, next of kin, or distributes of the decedent at the last known address of such person, within _____ days after the termination of such days' period. If the surviving partners elect to purchase the interest of the deceased partner in the said partnership, the purchase price, the method of payment, and the assets to be transferred shall be the same as previously stated herein with reference to the purchase of the interest of a retiring partner, except that in such event, the surviving partners shall be entitled to continue the use of the firm name of the partnership. All payments for the interest of said decedent in the said partnership shall be made to his duly appointed legal representative when he has been appointed and qualified. In the event that none has been appointed, the surviving partners shall at the time of service of notice hereinabove mentioned upon an heir at law, next of kin, or distributee of the decedent, at the same time serve upon him a demand that he cause such legal representative to be appointed. If such legal representative is not appointed at the time the surviving partners are to make such payment, it shall be extended until such legal representative has been appointed, and the surviving partners shall be entitled to hold the assets of the said partnership and use them in the conduct of the business thereof and shall be entitled to all profits received from the said business subsequent to the date of serving such notice.

17. If the surviving partners do not elect to purchase the interest of the decedent in the partnership, they shall proceed with reasonable diligence to liquidate the business of the partnership. Procedure as to liquidation and distribution of the business of the partnership shall be the same as previously stated for the liquidation of the business in case of the retirement of one of the partners.

IN WITNESS WHEREOF, the parties hereto have hereunto set their hands and seals the day and year first above written.

_____   _____
(Witnesses, if any)   (Signatures)

_____   _____
                                 _____
                                 _____

FORM 22: Partnership Agreement Between Father and Son/Daughter

This Agreement made and entered into this _____ day of _____, 19 ____, by and between _____ and _____, both of the City of _____, County of _____, State of_____, witnesseth:

That the above-named and undersigned parties do hereby form a partnership for the purpose of carrying on a _____ business, to be a continuation of the _____ business heretofore owned and operated by_____, one of the parties hereto, for which purpose the undersigned have agreed to the following terms and conditions, to the faithful performance of which they bind themselves each to the other, their heirs, executors, and administrators:

1. Name and Term: The name and style of the partnership shall be _____, and it shall continue until the mutual consent of the partners to dissolve, subject to the provisions herein set forth.

2. Interest of Partners: The interest in the business shall be held by the above-named parties in the following proportions, that is to say:

Name	*Percentage*

3. Management:_____is to have full and complete charge of the operation of the business, and shall have the sole authority to invest funds, purchase equipment, hire, and discharge employees in his full discretion, and to in all respects manage the conduct and operation of the business at all times as he may see fit.

4. Distribution of Profits: The net profits arising from the operation of the business shall be divided between the partners in proportion to their respective interests herein set out, but shall be payable only at such times as_____may in his discretion designate, and he shall have the right within his discretion to permit the net profits, or any part of the same,

to accumulate and remain in the business until such time as in his discretion he thinks it proper to pay over the same to the partners in proportion to their respective interests, and all losses incurred, whether from bad debts, depreciation of goods, or any other cause, and all expenses of the business shall be borne by the partners in the following proportions, that is to say:

Name	*Percentage*

5. Salaries of Partners: _____ shall receive for his services for managing the business the sum of not more than _____ dollars ($_____) per month, and such sums so drawn shall be charged as an operating expense and deducted before any division of the profits is made.

6. Purchase of Interest: _____ shall have the right at any time during the existence of this partnership to purchase the interest of _____ upon demand at the then book value of such interest in the business, after deducting any obligation which might then be due and owing by ____ to the partnership, and upon such purchase and payment as aforesaid the interest of _____ in the partnership shall immediately cease and terminate.

7. Disposal of Interest: _____ shall not sell or dispose of his/her interest in the partnership to any third party, but if _____ should desire to dispose of his/her interest in the partnership and retire therefrom, the right is reserved to _____ to purchase the interest of _____ in the partnership at its then book value, less any amount ____ may then owe the partnership.

8. Death of Partner: In the event of the death of either of the partners, the surviving partner shall have the right to purchase from the personal representatives of the deceased partner the interest of such deceased partner in the business at its then book value, such right or option to be exercised by surviving partner within six months from the death of such deceased partner.

9. Books and Accounts: All purchases, sales, transactions, and accounts of the partnership shall be kept in regular books which shall always be open to the inspection of the partners and their legal representatives, and at least once a year a statement shall be prepared showing the net profits of the partnership for the preceding year for the examination of the partners.

Whereas, a verbal agreement was entered into between the undersigned effective as of _____, 19 ____, which verbal agreement contained the provisions and conditions herein set forth, and the partnership has actually been in operation under the verbal agreement since _____, 19 ____, and which verbal agreement has now been reduced to writing as herein set forth, it is understood and agreed with respect to the payment of the net profits arising from the operation of the partnership, the same shall relate back to the_____day of _____, 19____.

To the faithful performance of this Agreement, the undersigned do hereby bind themselves, their heirs, executors, and administrators.

_____   _____
(Witnesses, if any)   (Signatures)

_____   _____

FORM 23: Partnership Agreement Between Husband and Wife

This Agreement in writing, this day entered into by and between _____ and _____, husband and wife, witnesseth:

WHEREAS, the parties have engaged in the operation of the _____, hereinafter mentioned, for a long period of years; and

WHEREAS, certain parts of that business have been conducted in the name of _____, individually, and certain parts in the name of _____, individually; and

WHEREAS, certain of the properties used in the operation of the business are not now owned by the parties hereto on an equal basis; and

WHEREAS, it is the desire and intention of the parties to recognize the equal ownership of all of the properties, and the equal responsibility and authority for the management of the business; and

WHEREAS, it is the desire and intention of the parties to enter into this agreement, whereby the equal ownership, responsibility, and authority shall be maintained by the parties on a permanent basis;

NOW, THEREFORE, it is mutually understood and agreed between the parties hereto as follows:

The parties hereto shall be equal partners in the ownership and operation of the _____ conducted under the trade name of_____all of which business is now being conducted by the parties in the City of _____, State of _____, and elsewhere, with the general offices located at _____, City of _____, State of _____.

The assets of the partnership, to be equally owned by the parties, shall include the following:

All office equipment, motor vehicles, supplies, and miscellaneous equipment of all kinds used in the operation of the business.

All accounts receivable of the business and all cash on hand and in banks.

All inventories of furniture and other merchandise on hand at the company offices in _____, _____, and elsewhere.

All real estate owned by the undersigned, including the building and lands located at _____ and _____ in the City of _____, State of _____.

Appropriate deeds of conveyance shall be executed to effect the equal ownership of the real properties.

The parties shall, from time to time by mutual consent, divide the duties and responsibilities of management of the affairs of the partnership.

The parties shall have an equal interest in the assets of the partnership, and shall share equally in the profits and losses of the business now conducted or hereafter to be conducted by the partnership. It is recognized and agreed that this division of ownership and this division of responsibility and authority embodied in this Agreement is entered into by the parties for the purpose of insuring the stability of the operation of the business and the personal and business affairs of the operation of the business and the personal and business affairs of the parties. In order to accomplish this purpose, it is understood and agreed that this Agreement shall of necessity be permanent, and that it shall not be altered or terminated as long as the undersigned shall remain husband and wife, and that if the parties shall at any time be legally separated or divorced, this Agreement shall thereupon be terminated, and the assets of the partnership divided equally between the parties, and that such division shall constitute a final and complete division of the property and property rights of the undersigned, and shall be in lieu of all other claims between the parties for separate maintenance, alimony, or otherwise.

In the event of the dissolution of the partnership during the lifetime of the parties, and one party desires to continue the operation of the business, such partner shall have the right to purchase the interest of the retiring partner in the assets of the partnership, and to defer the payment of the purchase price therefor over a period of five years from the date of such dissolution.

Witness our signatures, in duplicate, on this _____ day of _____, 19 ____.

_____   _____

(Witnesses, if any)   (Signatures)

_____   _____

FORM 24: Partnership Agreement for the Operation of Real Estate and Insurance Business

This Agreement, made this _____ day of __, 19 ____, by and between _____, hereafter called first party, and _____, hereafter called the second party, witnesseth:

1. Business: That the second party has acquired an undivided one-half interest in the real estate and insurance business heretofore owned and conducted by the first party, with office and place of business located at   _____, _____.

2. Firm Name: That the parties hereby agree to continue the operation of that business as partners under the assumed name and style of _____, the partnership to continue for an indefinite time and until terminated as herein provided or as may be mutually agreed upon.

3. Capital: That the amount of capital contributed to the partnership by the parties is hereby agreed to be the sum of dollars ($_____) each, and is represented by the following personal property, to wit: *(list each item)*

4. Reserve of Profits: It is hereby agreed that an additional sum of _____ dollars ($_____) shall be set up and reserved from the profits of the business, and shall become and be a part of the invested capital, it being agreed that not less than _____ percent of the net earnings shall be so reserved until that amount is accumulated.

5. Deposit of Funds: That the capital funds of the partnership, and all other moneys of the partnership, shall be deposited in the name of the partnership in the _____ Bank, and all trust funds shall be deposited in the bank in a separate account, and all such funds, partnership or trust, shall be subject to withdrawal only by check made in the name of the partnership and signed by either partner.

6. Attention of Partners: That each partner shall devote all his time and attention to the business of the partnership, and shall not, directly or indirectly, engage in any other business without the consent of the other partner.

7. Accounts: That full and accurate accounts of the transactions of the partnership shall be kept in proper books, and each partner shall cause to be entered in the books full and accurate accounts of all his transactions on behalf of the partnership. The books shall be kept at the place of business of the partnership, and each party shall at all times have access to and may inspect and copy any of them.

8. Withdrawals: Each party shall be entitled to draw such amounts and at such times, from the partnership earnings, as shall from time to time be fixed and agreed upon.

9. Annual Account: That at the end of each calendar year, a full and accurate inventory shall be prepared, and the assets, liabilities, and income, both gross and net, shall be ascertained, and the net profits or net losses of the partnership shall be fixed and determined. The net profits or net losses shall be divided equally between the parties hereto, and the account of each shall be credited or debited with his proportionate share thereof.

10. Outside Obligations: That neither party shall, without the written consent of the other, make, execute, deliver, endorse, or guarantee any commercial paper, nor agree to answer for, or indemnify against, any act, debt, default, or miscarriage of any person, partnership, association, or corporation, other than that of the parties hereto.

11. Termination: That the partnership may be terminated by either party upon giving sixty (60) days' notice to the other party of his desire to withdraw, in which event an accounting shall be had and a division of the partnership assets made, provided, however, that the party to whom the notice is given shall have the right to acquire the whole interest of the partnership at a price not to exceed the book value thereof, on such terms as may be agreed upon, and to continue the business under the same business name.

IN WITNESS WHEREOF, we have executed this Agreement this _____ day of _____, 19 ____.

_____   _____

(Witnesses, if any)   (Signatures)

FORM 25: Partnership Agreement Between Inventor and Promoter

This Agreement made this _____ day of _____, 19____, between _____, first party, and _____, second parties, witnesseth:

WHEREAS, on or about the _____ day of ____, 19____, the parties of the second part did apply through _____, patent attorneys, for letters of patent on a certain device known as the_____, being Application Number_____, United States Patent Office; and

WHEREAS, it is the desire of the parties of the second part to procure financial assistance from party of the first part for the purpose of exploiting and promoting the manufacture and sale of the device, and also territorial rights for the promotion and sale of the device when and if patent rights have been issued:

NOW, THEREFORE, it is agreed:

Party of the first part agrees to loan to parties of the second part, from time to time, various sums of money, which sums shall not exceed a total of _____ dollars ($_____), in the following manner:

In consideration of all and singular the above, parties of the second part do hereby transfer, assign, set over, and sell to party of the first part a _____ percent interest in and to any and all contracts, profits, or benefits derived from the exploitation or sale of the device, or from the sale of any territorial rights appertaining thereto, including the _____ percent interest in and to any and all patent rights now pending in the United States Patent Office, as well as in and to all rights to any improvement thereon hereafter obtained.

It is further agreed by and between the parties hereto that, as advances of funds are made, parties of the second part will, at the option of the party of the first part, secure the same either by promissory notes executed by parties of the second part or by the deposit with party of the first part of contracts for the sale of the device, it being understood that any and all funds or receipts derived from the same of the device, or

from the sale of territorial rights appertaining thereto shall
be collected by party of the first part, and the party of the
first part shall have the right to retain any and all funds collected on the contracts and to apply the same in repayment
of all sums theretofore advanced.

It is further understood and agreed that parties of the second part shall retain full control of the management and operation of the business, subject, however, to the rights of the party
of the first part, as hereinabove set forth. In being understood
and agreed that it is the desire of all parties hereto to exploit
and promote the sale and distribution of the device, and to
this end all parties agree to lend their best efforts. However,
the party of the first part shall not be required to render service other than as herein set forth.

This Agreement shall be binding upon the successors, heirs,
executors, administrators, and assigns of the respective parties hereto.

IN WITNESS WHEREOF, the parties have hereunto set
their hands the day and year first above written:

_____   _____
(Witnesses, if any)   (Signatures)

_____   _____

FORM 26: Limited Partnership Agreement

We, the undersigned, being desirous of forming a limited partnership, pursuant to the laws of this state do hereby certify:

1. The name of the firm under which said partnership is to be conducted is _____.

2. The character of the business intended to be transacted by said partnership is as follows:_____.

3. The location of the principal place of business is to be at

_____.

4. The name and place of residence of each general partner interested in said partnership is as follows: _____.

5. The name and place of residence of each limited partner interested in said partnership is as follows:_____.

6. The time at which said partnership is to begin business is__, and the time at which said partnership is to end is__.

7. The amount of cash and a description of and the agreed value of the other property contributed by each general partner is as follows: _____.

8. The additional contributions agreed to be made by each general partner and the time at which the event on the happening of which they shall be made is as follows: _____.

9. The time agreed upon when the contributions of each general partner are to be returned is as follows: _____.

10. The share of the profits or the other compensation by way of income which each general partner shall receive by reason of his contribution is as follows:_____.

11. The amount of cash and a description of the agreed value of the other property contributed by each limited partner is as follows: _____.

12. The additional contributions agreed to be made by each limited partner and the time at which the event on the happening of which they shall be made is as follows: _____.

13. The share of the profits or the other compensation by way of income which each limited partner shall receive by reason of his contribution is as follows:_____.

14. The right of a limited partner to substitute an assignee as contributor in his place, and the terms and conditions of the substitution, are as follows: _____.

15. The right of the partners to admit additional limited partners is as follows:_____.

16. The right of one or more of the limited partners to priority over other limited partners, as to contributions or as to compensation by way of income, and the nature of such priority are as follows: _____.

17. The right of the remaining general partner or partners to continue the business on the death, retirement, or insanity of a general partner is as follows: _____.

18. The right of a limited partner to demand and receive property other than cash in return for his contribution is as follows:_____.

Date:_____

_____   _____
(Witnesses)   General Partner

_____   _____
                                 General Partner

_____   _____
                                 Limited Partner

_____   _____
                                 Limited Partner

FORM 27: Joint Venture for Purchase and Sale of Tract of Land

This Agreement, entered into this _____ day of _____, 19____, between_____, and_____, witnesseth:

WHEREAS, the parties have purchased and are the owners in common of the following described real estate: ____; and

WHEREAS, the property is being purchased under contract for _____ dollars ($_____) payable as follows:_____; and

WHEREAS, _____is to furnish the money for the purchase, and the legal title of the land is to be held by him;

NOW, THEREFORE, it is hereby mutually agreed by and between the parties hereto, that the proceeds realized from the sale of the real estate when sold, together with the income, if any, from the real estate, after payment of taxes and all costs of every kind and nature, shall be applied as follows: _____ percent to _____; _____ percent to _____; and should any loss be incurred by reason of the purchase of the real estate, such loss shall be borne _____ percent by __, and _____ percent by_____.

It is further agreed that the best efforts shall be made by all parties hereto, to accomplish the sale of the land, and when a profit of _____ percent or more can be obtained, parties hereto shall agree to a sale. Unless profits from sales, or income from the property, shall be sufficient to carry taxes, interest and charges, and insurance at the end of _____ years from this date and thereafter, it is understood that _____ will carry _____ percent, and _____ will carry _____ percent of such sums after the _____ year period has expired.

IN WITNESS WHEREOF, we have executed this Agreement this _____ day of _____, 19____.

_____   _____
(Witnesses, if any)   (Signatures)

FORM 28: Joint Venture for Construction of Apartment

This Agreement made the _____ day of _____, 19___, by and between _____ of the first part, and _____ of the second part, witnesseth:

WHEREAS, first party is the owner in fee simple of the following described property: _____; and

WHEREAS, the first party is about to begin the erection of an apartment house thereon, hereafter referred to as the improvements;

NOW, THEREFORE, in consideration of the premises and of the agreements therein, and for other good and valuable considerations, the receipt whereof is hereby confessed and acknowledged, it is agreed by and between the parties as follows:

Second party is to furnish all plans and specifications and pay all charges for the superintendency necessary in the erection of the improvements.

On the completion of the improvements by the first party, the building is to be offered for sale at the best price obtainable, and when sold, the parties hereto are to participate equally in the sale price, after first party has deducted the cost of the low and the net cost of the improvements.

In the event the improvements are not sold forthwith after completion, then the premises are to be rented, and the net income of the improvements and rentals is to be applied to a sinking fund controlled by both parties to this Agreement, and it is to be applied from time to time as the same matures on taxes, expenses, debts, and claims of every kind and nature against the premises until the same is completely paid out and the property stands free and clear of all taxes, liens, encumbrances, debts, or claims of any kind or nature whatsoever.

And it is agreed that there shall be no division of any moneys received from such income and rentals until the same is completely paid for, as herein in this paragraph provided, except upon the written consent, signed by both of the parties hereto, and the agreement of division must be signed in duplicate and attached to the duplicate copies of this Agreement.

It is understood and agreed that the term "net income" referred to in the preceding paragraph hereof means and is defined as that income or rentals from the improvements which will remain after deductions are made for general taxes, interest charged on loans outstanding against the improvements, insurance, water, rent, and cost of upkeep of the improvements.

It is further understood that the parties hereto will necessarily expend various and sundry items of moneys for legal services, payment of special taxes and incidentals, and it is agreed that each party is to keep a strict account and render to the other itemized statements of such expenditures and receipts therefor, and that the respective amounts are to be charged against the gross income of the premises at the completion thereof, and each party is to be reimbursed for all expenditures so made.

Time is of the essence hereof in every particular, and the covenants and agreements herein shall be binding upon and insure to the benefits of the heirs, executors, administrators, and assigns of the repsective parties hereto.

IN WITNESS WHEREOF, we have hereunto signed this Agreement this _____ day of _____, 19____.

_____   _____
(Witnesses, if any)   (Signatures)

_____   _____

FORM 29: Sale of Partnership Interest to Co-partners

This Agreement made and entered into this _____ day of _____, 19___, by and between _____ and _____, witness and agree:

WHEREAS, the above-named parties are at present engaged in the business known as _____, as partners under a certain agreement in writing, dated _____, 19___, and

WHEREAS, _____ has proposed to buy out the interest of _____ in said partnership, for the sum of _____ dollars, and _____ has agreed to sell to _____ his interest in said partnership for said amount if the conditions hereinafter stated are complied with.

IT IS HEREBY AGREED AS FOLLOWS:

1. _____, for and in consideration of the sum of _____ dollars, paid to him by _____, receipt of which is hereby acknowledged, does hereby assign, sell, and transfer unto _____, all of his interest in and to said partnership business, including his interest in all of the furniture, equipment, and furnishings of said business, stock of merchandise of said business, accounts receivable of said business, moneys in said business, and all of his right, title, and interest in and to any and all of the assets of whatsoever kind or nature, of the _____ company.

2. It is agreed that _____ shall and does assume and agree to pay all of the outstanding debts and obligations of the said partnership business, and to perform all of the covenants of the leases on the said premises, and to perform all other outstanding contracts and agreements required to be performed by said partnership; and _____ agrees to save and hold harmless _____ against any claim or claims that may arise by reason of the aforesaid debts, obligations, or covenants, or of any other claims, except those mentioned in the following paragraph.

3. _____ hereby warrants and represents that he has incurred no debts, nor contracted any obligations, nor has

he incurred any liability in the name of the partnership, or for which the partnership would be liable, other than such debts, obligations, or liabilities as are disclosed in the books of the partnership, or of which he has advised _____; and _____ agrees to save and hold harmless _____ on account of any claims that may be made against said partnership because of any debts, obligations, or liabilities which _____ incurred in the name of the partnership or which the partnership has become liable for on account of any act of _____, as to which _____ has failed or neglected to inform_____.

4._____agrees to prepare Federal Partnership Income Tax Returns for the partnership business from _____, 19____ to this date, and to supply _____ with a copy thereof. It is agreed that each of the parties hereto shall pay their individual income taxes on the income received from said partnership business.

5. All other tax obligations (including occupational taxes, personal property taxes, and various municipal licensing fees) shall be considered as obligations of the partnership, and are hereby assumed by _____.

6. It is agreed that the partnership heretofore existing between the parties hereto be, and the same is, hereby dissolved, and that this Agreement constitutes a full and complete accounting and liquidation of said partnership business, and, excepting as herein otherwise provided, _____ acknowledges that he has no claim or demand of whatsoever kind or nature against_____, and, except as herein otherwise provided, _____acknowledges that he has no claim or demand of whatsoever kind or nature against_____.

IN WITNESS WHEREOF, the parties hereto have signed this Agreement.

_____   _____

(Witnesses, if any)   (Signatures)

FORM 30: Dissolution Agreement

This Agreement made this _____ day of _____, 19____, by and between_____and_____, witness and agree:

That whereas, the parties to this agreement have heretofore conducted a partnership under the firm name and style of
_____; and

WHEREAS, _____ is desirous of withdrawing from said partnership and both the parties thereto have agreed and do agree that said partnership shall be dissolved and terminated; and

WHEREAS, _____ has this day conveyed to _____ all his interest in the real estate and certain of the personal property heretofore owned by said partnership upon the agreement that the assets of said partnership shall be promptly liquidated and said partnership terminated and closed.

NOW, THEREFORE, it is mutually agreed that the partnership heretofore existing between the parties to this Agreement, shall be liquidated and dissolved at as early a date as the same can be practically accomplished without loss to the parties in interest and the net assets realized, after paying all debts and expenses of liquidating the assets and caring for the property in the partnership, shall be divided equally between the parties hereto.

IN WITNESS WHEREOF, the parties hereto have signed this Agreement.

_____   _____
(Witnesses, if any)   (Signatures)

_____   _____

FORM 31: Notice of Dissolution

Notice is hereby given that the partnership heretofore existing between _____ and _____, under the fictitious name and style of _____ Company, located at _____, _____, _____, was dissolved by mutual consent, on the _____ day of _____, 19____.

_____ has withdrawn from and has ceased to be associated in the carrying on of said business, and ____ will hereafter carry on said business and he is entitled to all of the assets, including all debts due to said partnership, and has assumed and will pay all outstanding business obligations of_____Company heretofore and hereafter incurred.

_____   _____

(Signatures)

_____   _____

FORM 32: Notice under Fictitious Name Law

Notice is hereby given that the undersigned desiring to engage in business at _____ under the name of _____ Company, intend to register the said name with the Clerk and Recorder of _____ County.

_____   _____

Date   (Signatures)

_____   _____

FORM 33: Buy and Sell Agreement Between Two Parties

Agreement made this _____ day of _____, 19____, between _____, who resides at _____, and _____, who resides at _____.

_____and_____are partners doing business in the partnership known as _____. The interest of each partner in said partnership is set forth as follows:

_____ has _____ percent
_____ has _____ percent

The purpose of this Agreement is to provide for the purchase of the decedent's interest in said partnership by the survivor.

It is, therefore, mutually agreed by_____and_____ as follows:

Neither _____ nor _____ shall during their joint lives, assign, encumber, or dispose of any portion of their respective partnership interests in the __ _____ Company, by sale or otherwise, without the written consent of the other partner.

2. Upon the death of either partner, the survivor shall purchase, and the estate of the decedent shall sell, the partnership interest then owned by the partner who is first to die. The purchase price of such interest shall be computed in accordance with the provisions of paragraph 3 of this Agreement.

3. Unless and until changed as hereinafter provided, the total value of_____, for the purpose of determining the purchase price to be paid for the interest of a deceased partner, shall be_____dollars, and the value of each partner's interest in said partnership shall be as follows:

The interest of _____ shall be _____ dollars
The interest of _____ shall be _____ dollars

(a) The said purchase price includes an amount mutually agreed upon as representing the goodwill of the partnership as a going concern.

(b) Within _____ days following the end of each fiscal year, _____ and _____ shall redetermine the value of said partnership and their respective interests therein. Such values shall be endorsed on Schedule A, attached hereto. If_____and_____fail to determine said values for a particular year, the last previously stipulated values shall control, except that if no valuation is agreed upon for two consecutive years, the value of a partner's interest shall be determined by the independent, certified public accountant regularly retained by the partnership for the auditing of its books. If there is no such public accountant available, or if he fails to make a determination of such valuation, then the value shall be determined by any other accountant who may be selected by mutual agreement of the surviving partner, and the representative of the deceased partner.

(c) The surviving partner shall be entitled to all the profits of the business and suffer all the losses arising between the date of death of the deceased partner and the consummation of the sale of the interest of the deceased partner.

4. The purchase price shall be payable as follows: Not less than _____ dollars in cash, or the entire purchase price in cash if less than said amount, and if any balance of the purchase price remains unpaid, it shall be covered by a series of promissory notes of equal amounts payable to the order of the executors or administrators of the deceased partner, the first note maturing in _____, the second in _____, and the final one in _____, with interest on each note at the rate of _____ percent per annum, to be paid when each promissory note comes due on the unpaid balance. The surviving partner may elect to pay more than the specified amount in cash, may elect to have notes for a shorter period, and may pay any note in advance of its due date. The executors or administrators of the seller may agree to more liberal terms, such as a smaller amount of the purchase in cash, or notes for a longer period, or at a lower rate of interest, and may extend notes or waive any defaults, if they determine any such action to the best interest of the estate and the heirs and legatees of the deceased partner.

5. If notes are given in partial payment of the agreed purchase price, they shall be secured by a chattel mortgage on the tangible assets of the partnership of a value of _____ times the amount of the notes. All notes of the surviving partner shall forthwith fall due in event of default in payment of interest or principal of any note of said surviving partner.

6. The surviving partner shall pay and discharge all liabilities of the partnership existing at the date of the deceased partner's death, and shall save and keep the estate of the deceased partner free and relieved from any and all liability, either to the partnership or to any of the creditors of the partnership, and shall indemnify the deceased partner's estate against all costs, losses, and damages sustained or paid by the representatives of the estate in respect of partnership liabilities.

7. The surviving partner and the executors or administrators of the deceased partner shall make, execute, and deliver any document necessary to transfer ownership of the partnership assets and to carry out this Agreement.

8. This Agreement may be altered, amended, or terminated by a writing by both partners.

9. This Agreement shall terminate on the occurrence of any of the following events:

(a) Bankruptcy, receivership, or dissolution of the partnership;

(b) Bankruptcy, or insolvency of either partner;

(c) Death of both partners simultaneously or within a period of thirty days;

(d) Termination of the partnership business.

10. This Agreement shall be binding upon the partners, their heirs, legal representatives, successors, and assigns.

IN WITNESS WHEREOF, the parties hereto have executed this Agreement this _____ day of _____, 19____.

_____   _____
(Witnesses, if any)   (Signatures)

_____   _____

SCHEDULE A—Endorsements

Pursuant to Article 3 of this Agreement, the parties do hereby determine that the total value of the partnership business as of this _____ day of _____, 19____, and the value of each partner's respective interest is: _____

Alternative, Additional, and Supplemental Provisions for Partnership Agreements

There may be some occasions where additional provisions are desirable in an agreement or where further facts or details are needed to make the intention of the parties clear. You should use your discretion in determining whether, how, and to what extent, you utilize these clauses or parts of them to make your agreement complete. You should be careful not to use clauses on the same subject matter which may be inconsistent, contradictory, or indefinite.

Purpose Clauses

Sample 1:
The purpose of the partnership shall be the buying, selling, and exchanging of_____and the doing of all things necessary and incidental thereto.

Sample 2:
The partnership shall be for the purpose of carrying on the business of manufacturing and selling of _____ other items related thereto of whatsoever kind or character.

Sample 3:
The business of the partnership shall be as follows:
(1) To establish, maintain, conduct, and engage in the business of building and manufacturing of _____.
(2) To establish, maintain, conduct, and engage in the business of designing, developing, and drafting of plans, specifications, and designs for _____.
(3) To manufacture, build, and assemble such articles as
_____ .
(4) To buy, sell, hold, and convey such equipment, machinery, fixtures, and other personal property as may be necessary for the operation of the business herein contemplated by this partnership agreement.

Conduct of Business and Authority of Partners

Sample 1:

Equal Authority to Conduct Business: Each partner shall have an equal right in the management of the partnership business, and a decision by the majority shall be binding upon the partnership. However, no partner shall contract in the name and on the credit of the partnership in excess of____ dollars without the consent of all the partners.

Sample 2:

Management: _____ shall be the manager of said partnership and shall be authorized to sign all notes, checks, drafts, and other obligations and to execute all papers, under seal or otherwise. Further, he shall be in full charge of all business operations of said partnership for the purpose of carrying out the provisions of this Agreement. All decisions affecting the policy and management of the partnership, including the drawing accounts and compensation of partners and the control of employment, compensation, and discharge of employees shall be made on behalf of the partnership upon the approval of a majority of the partners.

Sample 3:

Meetings of Partners: For the purpose of discussing matters of general interest to the partnership, together with the conduct of its business, partners shall meet each _____ of each week, at _____ o'clock in the morning, or at such other time agreed upon by a majority of the partners. All meetings shall be decided by a majority vote of the partners, except that no change shall be made in the nature or scope of the partnership business, nor shall any act be done which would make it impossible to carry out the ordinary business of the partnership business, nor shall any change be made in this partnership agreement except with the consent of all the partners.

Deposit of Money

All moneys which shall from time to time be received for or on account of said partnership, not required for current expenses, shall be deposited immediately in the bank for the time being dealt with by the partnership, in the same drafts, checks, bills, or cash in which the same are received, and all disbursements for or on account of the partnerhip shall be made by check on such bank.

Expense Accounts

Each partner shall be entitled to an expense account of not to exceed_____dollars per week, of his actual, reasonable, and necessary expenses, incurred for and in behalf of the firm, but shall keep an itemized account thereof, which account shall only bind the other members thereof, when approved in writing by at least a majority of the partners. All such accounts shall be filed, after such approval, and kept for a period of at least one year after such approval.

Time to Be Devoted to Firm

Each partner shall devote his whole time and attention to the partnership business, and diligently and faithfully employ himself therein, and carry on the same to the greatest advantage of the partnership.

Bond

Each member of this partnership shall enter into a bond in the sum of _____ dollars, satisfactory to all of his partners hereunder, to the effect that he shall fully account to the said partnerhip for all property of the said firm which shall come to his possession, and that he will turn the same over to said firm.

Vacations

Each partner shall be entitled to _____ weeks vacation in each year. In the first year of the partnership, the said __ shall have the first choice of the time at which he shall take his vacation, and in all succeeding years the choice shall be made by the partners alternately.

Engaging in Other Business

No partner shall, during the continuance of the partnership, carry on or be concerned or interested, directly or indirectly, in the same kind of business as that carried on by said partnership, nor be engaged in or undertake any other trade, or business, without the consent in writing of the other partners or partner.

Managing Partner

The said _____ shall be the manager of the said business, and shall be paid for his services as manager the annual sum of_____dollars before any division of profits is made, and in addition thereto his share of the profits, by equal quarterly payments, the first salary payment to be made on the _____ day of _____, 19____.

Devotion to Business

Sample 1:
It is agreed by the parties to this Agreement, that at all times during the continuance of their partnership, they and each of them will give their attention and attendance, and to the utmost of their skill and power will exert themselves for their joint interest, profit, benefit, and advantage.

Sample 2:

It is agreed by and between the parties hereto, that at all times during the continuance of the partnership, each partner shall give reasonable time, attention, and attendance to, and use reasonable endeavors in, the business of the partnership, and shall, with reasonable skill and power, exert himself for the joint interest, profit, and advantage of the partnership.

Maintenance and Availability of Records

Sample 1:

Each of the partners may have access at all times to the books, papers, and records of the partnership, and may have them audited and examined by auditors, accountants, or attorneys at the sole and entire expense of the partner desiring the audit or examination.

Sample 2:

Books of accounts shall be kept and entries made therein of all moneys, goods, effects, debts, sales, purchases, receipts, payments, and all other writings belonging to the said partnership, shall be kept where the business of the partnership shall be carried on, and shall be at all times open to the examination of each partner.

Sample 3:

It is understood and agreed that there shall be kept at all times a complete set of books of account wherein there shall be entered any and all records and transactions of said business and that every month from the date hereof after the payment of all expenses of said partnership, including interest on the capital invested herein, and also at the expiration or other termination hereof, and books shall be balanced and a balance sheet shall be delivered to each partner showing the profits or losses from said partnership, as the same shall have been accurately ascertained, and such profits shall be shared by and divided between and credited to such losses borne by and charged to said partners in the proportions hereinabove set forth, and thereupon each partner shall be permitted to draw out his share of the profits, if any, so credited.

Management by Individual Partner

It is understood and agreed by and between the said partners that _____ shall be, and is from this date on, made the general manager of said partnership, that he shall be in full charge of all business operations of said partnership, and that he shall have the full right to conduct the business of said partnership in such manner as he may desire, including the selling of any and all of the partnership assets and the purchasing of such other property as he may desire in the name of the partnership together with the right to borrow such money as he may deem necessary to carry on said business.

Method of Resolving Differences

In the event of any misunderstanding between the partners concerning the matter of conducting and carrying on said business, the partners shall adjust the same between themselves. It is understood, however, in this connection that the decision of the general manager and one other partner hereto shall determine any question which may arise between them and in the event that any one or more of said partners should be dissatisfied with such decision, then they shall have the right as given them by the laws of the State of _____ to bring proceedings in court for the purpose of either dissolving the said partnership or obtaining such relief as they are entitled to under the terms of this partnership agreement.

Arbitration of Disputes

Sample 1:
If any disagreement shall arise between the partners in respect to the conduct of the business of the partnership, or its dissolution, or in respect to any other cause, matter, or thing whatsoever not otherwise provided for in the aforesaid partnership agreement, the same shall be decided and determined by one arbitrator, to wit: _____, and the decision of said arbitrator shall be binding and conclusive on the parties hereto.

Sample 2:
In the event that any dispute should arise concerning any of the terms, convenants, or conditions of this Agreement, or with respect to the enforcement thereof, or with respect to any dissolution or liquidation of the partnership, or with respect to any matter affecting the operation and conduct of the business of the partnership, such dispute shall be disposed of by arbitration by submitting the same to the American Arbitration Association in accordance with the rules and regulations of that association then obtaining, and in accordance with the laws of the State of _____.

Deposit and Withdrawal of Funds

Partnership moneys received from any and all sources shall be deposited in the name of the_____Company in the_____Bank, and shall be withdrawn therefrom only by check drawn and signed by _____.

Prohibition Against Commingling

All trust and other similar funds shall be deposited in another fund in the firm's name in another bank or trust company, and shall not be mingled with other moneys of the firm.

Control of Majority of Partners

The vote of a majority of the partners shall control any question that may come up for decision unless otherwise provided herein.

Right to Expel Partner

The right to terminate the interest of any one of the partners is hereby vested in the other partners for any cause which in their discretion seems to be reasonable, and the interests set forth hereinafter are accepted with this express condition and limitation.

Authority to Sign Checks and Written Instruments

It is understood and agreed that all checks to be drawn in the regular course of business of the firm shall be signed by _____. Checks of the firm shall be used only for the firm business and no account or charge against any of the partners shall be paid with a firm check. In the event it becomes necessary to borrow money and to execute any bills, notes, contracts, or agreements binding the firm or pledging the firm credit, the same must be executed by _____.

Restrictions on Powers of Partners

No partner shall, without the written consent of the others, enter into any bond or become an endorser or surety for any person, or knowingly cause or suffer to be done anything whereby the partnership property may be seized, attached, or taken on execution or endangered, nor shall such partner assign, mortgage, or charge his share of the assets of profits of the partnership, or any part of said share, or draw, accept, or endorse any bill of exchange or promissory note on account of the partnership.

Requirement of Countersignature of Partner

No checks shall be drawn or vouchers issued unless signed by at least two parties to this Agreement.

Requirements of Mutual Assent to Guaranties

None of the partners, during the continuance of this partnership, shall assume any liability for another or others, by means of endorsement or of becoming guarantor or surety, without first obtaining the consent of the other thereto in writing.

Covenant of Good Faith

Each of the parties hereto shall diligently employ himself in the business of said partnership, and be faithful to the other in all transactions relating to the same, and give, whenever required, a true account of all business transactions arising out of, or connected with, the conduct of the partnership, and neither of the parties shall engage in any business except that of the said partnership or on account thereof, and neither shall, without the written conent of the other, employ either the capital or credit of the partnership in any other than partnership business.

Indemnification Against Partner's Separate Debts

Sample 1:
Neither party shall do or suffer to be done anything whereby the capital or the property of the partnership may be attached or taken in execution, and each partner shall punctually pay his separate debts and indemnify the other partners and the capital and property of the partnership against the same.

Sample 2:
Each partner shall promptly pay his debts, and keep indemnified the other partners, and the stock-in-trade, capital, and property of the partnership, against the same, and all expenses on account thereof.

Sample 3:
Each partner shall at all times duly and punctually pay and discharge his separate and private debts and engagements whether present or future and keep indemnified therefrom and from all actions, claims, and demands in respect thereof, the partnership property.

Restriction on Engaging in Other Enterprises

Neither of the partners shall, during the term, use the trade or business of the firm, as aforesaid, for his private benefit or advantage; but shall, at all times, do his best by all lawful means to the utmost of his skill and power, for the joint interest, profit, benefit, and advantage of the firm.

Partnership Right to Patents and Trade Secrets

Any ideas that may be the subject of application for letters patent and trade secrets or formulas discovered by either of the parties during the course of the partnership shall become partnership property.

Admission of Sons or Daughters into Firm

Either of said partners may at any time nominate a son/daughter, being of the age of twenty-one years or more, to succeed to his/her share in the partnership and the capital and future profits thereof; and upon signing a proper written contract respecting the admission of a new partner, every such son/daughter shall be and become a partner in the partnership concern in the place, and in respect of the share and interest, of his/her father/mother therein, and be entitled thereto upon the same terms and conditions, and under the subject to the same advantages, regulations, and agreements, in all respects and in the same manner, as the father/mother would have been entitled to if he/she had remained a partner, or as near thereto as the difference of circumstances will permit.

Rights and Duties Among Partners

The Uniform Partnership Act sets out in considerable detail the rules determining the rights and duties of partners toward each other. But you will remember that these rights and duties may be altered by agreement among the partners. Among the rights specifically set out in the Uniform Act are the rights of each partner:

- to share equally in the profits of the firm
- to receive repayment of his contribution
- to receive indemnification for payments made on behalf of the firm
- to receive interest on advances and, under certain circumstances, on capital contributions
- to share in the management and conduct of the business
- to have access to the firm's books
- to have a formal account of partnership affairs

These rights are complemented by certain duties:

- to contribute toward losses sustained by the firm
- to work for the partnership without remuneration
- to submit to a majority vote when differences arise among partners as to the conduct of the firm's business
- to disclose to other partners any information a partner has regarding partnership matters
- to account to the firm for any profit derived by the partner from any partnership transaction or from the use of partnership property

The rule that partners have a fiduciary duty to other partners extends to the partnership and each partner has the obligation of maintaining the utmost good faith and integrity in his or her dealings with the partnership and the partnership affairs. It is a fundamental characteristic of the partnership that the relation existing between the partners is one of trust and confidence when dealing with each other in relation to partnership matters. Each partner is, in one sense, a trustee. The same rules and tests are applied to the conduct of partners as are ordinarily applicable to trustees and agents.

In applying these general statements, each partner has a right to know all that the others know about their business matters. Each is required to make full disclosure of all material facts within his or her knowledge in any way relating to the partnership affairs. One partner may not deceive another partner by the concealment of material facts. A partner, in acting for the partnership, must consult his or her partners in every important activity of the partnership affairs, in the absence of special circumstances excusing him or her from so doing.

The Uniform Act reinforces the above rules by providing that partners must render on demand true and full information of all things affecting the partnership to any partner or the legal representative of any deceased partner or any partner under legal disability. The duty imposed by the Uniform Act is owed by all partners, but the standard of rigid, fair dealing required of a managing partner to the inactive partners is especially high.

Power of Partners

The functions, rights, and duties of partners are based primarily on the principles of agency. In fact, the law of partnership is a branch of the law of agency, and it is universally recognized that the liability of one partner for the acts of his co-partners is founded on principles of agency. It follows that every partner, apart from any special powers conferred on him by the partnership agreement, is not only a principal, but is also, for all purposes within the scope and objects of the partnership, a general and authorized agent of the firm, and the agent of all the partners. This is the fundamental basis upon which you may be held liable and responsible for acts of your partners.

A partner virtually acts as principal for himself or herself and as agent for his or her partners, and for the partnership. During the existence of a partnership, therefore, each member is deemed to be authorized to transact the whole business for the firm, his or her acts being treated as the acts of all. If the partner has the requisite authority, he or she binds the partnership whether he or she acts in its name or his or her own name. The law presumes there is liability for a transaction entered into by a partner acting apparently within the scope of his or her authority. Evidence which might prove favorable for the other members of the partnership may include a showing that credit was given to the individual partner alone, or that it was known that such partner acted fraudulently or without the authority and consent of his or her partners, or any other facts to demonstrate a lack of liability.

Although not stated in so many words in the Uniform Act, one of the principal obligations of partners toward each other is to exercise the utmost good faith and maintain the highest integrity in dealing with each other.

Relations of Partner to the Partnership

The terms of a partnership agreement may expressly regulate the duty of the partners to render services to the firm. By these terms, partners often agree to perform work themselves during the continuance of the partnership for their mutual interest, profit, and advantage. In the absence of an agreement to the contrary, each partner is required to give to the firm all of his or her time, skill, and ability. It is also his or her duty to use his or her knowledge, skill, and diligence for the promotion of the common benefit of the business.

As stated in the Uniform Act, no partner is entitled to remuneration for acting in the partnership business, unless otherwise agreed by the partners. It goes on to state that a surviving partner is entitled to reasonable compensation for his or her services in winding up the partnership affairs. It is recognized that in managing partnership affairs, each partner is, in effect, taking care of his or her own interest or managing his or her own business, and is merely performing his or her own duties and obligations growing out of his or her role as a partner. For the rendering of such services he or she is not, in the absence of a contract, express or implied, entitled to compensation beyond his or her share of the profits.

Under the Uniform Act, as well as at common law, an individual partner can by his or her acts bind the partnership by entering into contracts with third parties within the limits allowed by the partnership agreement. This should encourage all partners to have a full and complete agreement in writing.

Property Rights of Partners

All property originally brought into the partnership stock or subsequently acquired by purchase or otherwise, on account of the partnership, is partnership property, and unless the contrary intention appears, property acquired with partnership funds is property of the partnership. Real estate may be acquired in the firm name and may be conveyed in the partnership name.

In contrast to its regulation of sales of real property, the Uniform Act does not specifically deal with sales of personal property. At common law dealing in personal property was also much less circumscribed than dealing in realty since personal property was generally recognized as being the property of the firm and not of individual partners.

Individual Rights of Partners in Partnership

The specific property rights of an individual partner in the partnership property, under the Uniform Act, include his or her rights in specific partnership property, his or her interest in the partnership, and his or her right to participate in the management of the business of the partnership. His or her interest in the partnership, by whatever name it may be called, is personal property. A partner is co-owner with his or her partners of specific partnership property holding as a tenant in partnership. The nature, incidents and characteristics of this tenancy in partnership are not always clear; however, the Uniform Act sets out, in some detail, a description of the property right.

In all discussions about the Uniform Act, it is emphasized that the act has been adopted in virtually all states in whole or in part, and that its rules apply in most instances only if there is not a written partnership agreement establishing some other specific arrangement.

Civil Liability of Partners

Since the rights and duties of partners are generally measured by the rules applicable to agency relationship, the liability of one partner for the acts of his or her partners is based on the rule that each one is an agent of every other. The Uniform Act prescribes the nature of the liability. With respect for the firm's liability for acts performed in its name and within the scope of its business, the partners are jointly liable for all debts and obligations of the partnership. Each partner is bound by admissions or representations made by any partner regarding partnership affairs. Such liability also extends to negligence, wrongful acts, and breach of trust by partners acting within the scope of the partnership business. This exposure to liability is the primary objection to conducting a business through a partnership arrangement.

Criminal Liability of Partners

A partnership can violate a criminal statute apart from the participation and knowledge of the partners as individuals, but the conviction of a partnership cannot be used to punish the individual partners, who might be completely free of personal guilt. The criminal conviction of a partnership as an entity can lead only to a fine levied on the firm's assets. The argument has been made that the words *knowingly* and *willfully* in a criminal statute eliminate partnership from the coverage of such statutes because a partnership, as opposed to its individual partners, cannot act knowingly and willfully. The United States Supreme Court has rejected this argument holding that, while partnerships as well as corporations and other associations cannot so act, it is elementary that such im-

personal entities can be guilty of knowing or willful violations
of regulatory statutes through the acts of its agents. The courts
reasoned that, if the partnership itself obtains the fruits of
the violations which are committed knowingly by agents of
the firm in the scope of their employment, the business entity cannot be left free to break the law merely because its
owners, that is, the partners, do not personally participate in
the legal activity.

The Uniform Act provides that where any wrongful act of
any partner acting in the ordinary course of business causes
loss or injury to any nonpartner, or where, as a result, any
penalty is incurred, the partnership is then liable to the same
extent as the individual partner. Consequently, a usury penalty
may be imposed against a partnership engaged in the loan
business or extending credit.

A partnership engaged in a lawful enterprise generally will
not cause one partner to be liable for the intentional criminal
act of another. There may be liability, however, if unlawful
acts are done with knowledge and consent of the partners. In
other words, while the partnership, as an entity, can be held
for the criminal acts of its agents, individual partners cannot
be convicted of willfully violating a criminal law without a
showing thaat they had knowledge of the criminal act of their
agent, or that they received and appropriated the benefit of
the act. But where a partner willfully participates in a violation of law, the fact that he, as well as the partnership, is in-
dicted does not constitute a violation of the constitutional pro-
hibition against double jeopardy.

Where guilty intent is an element of a crime, partners who
do not participate in a criminal act will not be held liable. Conversely, if all the partners participate in a criminal act, all are
guilty.

Dissolution of Partnership and Winding Up of Partnership Business

Although courts and lawyers are not always precise in distinguishing among the various terms which apply to that process which leads to the final settlement of all partnership affairs, the authors of the Uniform Act suggest the following delineation: Dissolution designates that point in time when the partners cease to carry on the business together; winding up, often called liquidation, is the process of settling partnership affairs after dissolution; and termination is the point in time when all the partnership affairs are wound up.

Dissolution of Partnership

The Uniform Act defines dissolution as the change in the relation of the partners caused by any partner ceasing to be associated in the carrying on of the business. Dissolution is not in itself a termination of the partnership or of the rights and powers of partners, for many of these persist during the winding up process. Rather, the term is descriptive of that change in the partnership relation which ultimately results in its termination.

Dissolution is caused either by operation of law or by judicial decree. Where the Uniform Act is in effect, the dissolution of a partnership can only be brought about as provided by the act. However, the courts have recognized that dissolution may

take place under certain circumstances not specifically
enumerated in the act. For example, the admission or
withdrawal of a partner from the firm has been held to result
in dissolution.

The dissolution of a partnership can be caused or required
by any number of things, including the following: by operation of law, termination of term or purpose, by will of one partner, by mutual consent, the admission of new partner, the
withdrawal or retirement of a partner, expulsion or exclusion
of a partner, assignment of a partner's interest in the partnership, assignment of a partner's property rights, sale or
transfer of firm effects, changes in personal status of partners,
bankruptcy or insolvency, and many others.

Winding Up of Business

Winding up means the administration of assets for the purpose of terminating the business and discharging the obligations of the partnership to its members. While the provisions
of the Uniform Act relating to the application of partnership
property on dissolution is concerned with a discontinuance of
the day-to-day business, it does not forbid other methods of
winding up a partnership. For example, a provision for withdrawal of a partner may be considered a type of winding up
of a partnership without the necessity of discontinuing the dai-
ly business.

The Uniform Act provides that unless otherwise agreed, the
partners who have not wrongfully dissolved the partnership,
or the legal representative of the last surviving partner, if not
bankrupt, have the right to wind up the partnership affairs.
Where dissolution is caused by the bankruptcy of a partner,
the power to wind up is vested in the nonbankrupt partner
unless there is a different agreement. Any partner, his legal
representative, or his assignee, upon dissolution, may file court
action to obtain winding up under court jurisdiction.

Where a partnership is ended by mutual consent or by the
expiration of its term, the right to wind up is vested in all the
partners. In that case, each partner is under a duty to liquidate
partnership affairs, which would include the performance of
existing contracts, the collection of debts or claims due the
firm, and the payment of firm debts.

The partners who have the right to wind up may agree that one or more of them shall act as liquidating partners. It requires no express authority to act as a liquidating partner after active operations of the firm have ceased, or after its dissolution. If a partner so acts with the knowledge of the other partners, their permission may be presumed. The partner who remains in charge of the business during the winding up period occupies a fiduciary relationship to the other partners until the winding up of the partnership affairs is complete. If the partners cannot agree as to who shall wind up, a receiver may be appointed by the court.

Accounting

One of the ordinary duties of partners is to keep true and correct books showing the firm accounts, such books being at all times open to the inspection of all the members of the firm. This duty primarily rests on the managing or active partner, and he or she cannot defeat the rights of his or her partner to a settlement and proper distribution of the assets by failing to keep the accounts. In fact, the managing partner will be held to strict proof of the items of his or her accounts. In determining whether the managing partner has properly performed the proper duties in keeping accounts, the court may consider the nature of the business, the intellectual ability of the partners, and the place and conditions under which the work is to be performed.

According to the Uniform Act the partnership books shall be kept, subject to any agreement between the partners, at the principal place of business of the partnership, and every partner shall at all times have access to and may inspect and copy any of them. This provision refers to an active partnership. When a partnership is dissolved, the firm books and records belong to all of the partners.

Application of Assets to Liabilities

In settling accounts between partners after dissolution, the Uniform Act states that the liabilities of the partnership rank in payment as follows:

First: those owed to creditors other than partners,

Second: those owed to partners other than for capital and profits,

Third: those owed to partners in respect of capital, and

Last: those owed to partners in respect to profits.

These statutory rules for distribution of assets are applicable only in the absence of an agreement between the partners specifying some other method of distribution.

After the payment of liabilities the surplus may be applied to the payment of the net amount owed to the partners. When a partner leaves the firm voluntarily, or involuntarily, without assigning his interest to the other partners or agreeing to continuation of the business, he or she is entitled to receive an amount equal to the value of his or her interest at dissolution. The same rule applies when a partner dies so that his or her representative may have the value of the deceased's interest at the date of dissolution.

Rights of Firm Creditors

It is clear that both under the Uniform Act and under the doctrine of marshalling of assets, the first rank in order of payment is for liabilities owed to creditors other than partners. All firm debts must be paid before any partner is entitled to any part of the firm assets. Each partner has the right to have the partnership property applied to the payment or security for the payment of partnership debts in order to relieve him or her from personal liability. Upon the death of a partner this right passes to his or her personal representative.

Rights of Partners

The second rank in order of payment is for those liabilities owed to partners other than for capital and profits. This provision is in accord with the general rule that in the absence of an agreement which will determine rights as to advances, each partner is a creditor of the firm as to money loaned it and has a right to repayment after the debts to other creditors have been met. The payment of interest on advances also falls within the second rank in order of payment if there is an express or implied agreement to pay interest.

The third rank in order of payment are those liabilities owed to partners in respect to capital. This is in accord with the general rule that after liability to third persons and firm debts to partners are paid, each partner is entitled to the repayment of the capital contributed by him or her. The fourth and last rank in order of payment are those liabilities owed to the partners in respect to profits. Each partner shall share equally in the profits and surplus remaining after all liabilities, including those to the partners, are satisfied. Unless there is an express or implied agreement to the contrary, the partners share equally in the profits, even though they may have contributed unequally to capital or services. The sharing of profits may be controlled by an express agreement between the parties, and an agreement may be implied from the course of conduct of the partners.

Rights of Separate Creditors

The Uniform Act provides that while partnership creditors have priority in regard to partnership assets, creditors of an individual partner have priority as to the individual property of that partner. Similarly, in applying the doctrine of marshalling assets the rule is recognized that creditors of the individual members of a partnership are entitled to preference over firm creditors in regard to the separate estates of the partners. The separate creditors may require firm creditors to exhaust their remedy against the firm before resorting to the property of its individual members. However, in some states, it has been held that after the partnership assets have been fully and fairly exhausted, partnership creditors are allowed to come in *pro rata* with the separate creditors.

Death of Partner

Unless the partners have previously agreed that dissolution would not occur, the death of a partner dissolves, by law, the partnership of which the deceased person was a member. The effect of death is to confer on the representatives of the deceased partner certain rights against the surviving partners and to impose upon the surviving partners certain corresponding obligations. The surviving partners and the representatives of the deceased partner may agree upon an adjustment of the partnership affairs upon any basis that they choose, and in the absence of mistake or fraud, this adjustment will be binding on all the parties to the agreement.

Sole Proprietorship

Part III

You As Sole Proprietor

You have learned how easy it is to form your own corporation and to prepare your own partnership agreements. Now, you come to the easiest part. The sole proprietorship is the oldest, simplest, and most prevalent form of business enterprise in America.

A sole proprietorship is a form of business in which one person owns all the assets of the business in contrast to a partnership or corporation. The sole proprietor is solely liable for all the debts of the business. The word *proprietary* is defined as "a proprietor or owner; one who has exclusive title to a thing in his or her own right; one who possesses the dominion or ownership of a thing in his or her own right."

Thus, it is easy to see that starting a small business as sole proprietor is a one-person operation. When additional people come into your business as owners, you will wish to consider the advisability of switching to a partnership or a corporation.

One of the distinctive characteristics of a sole proprietorship is that the owner has complete control of the business. Partnerships must have detailed and specific agreements as to who will make decisions and what mechanisms will be used when partners disagree. A corporation is controlled by a board of directors, and while it is generally governed by a majority vote of the directors, there have been many proxy fights among owners and shareholders of corporations. It cannot be as simple and easy as a business owned and controlled by one person.

A sole proprietorship is simple, convenient and the owner has absolute control in the management of the business. There is no necessity for articles of incorporation or agreements. In fact, there are virtually no formalities to start a business. If a business is engaged in the retail business a tax license from the state is necessary. However, this is required of any business. The same is true of occupational licenses where required by the state. There is no formal business organization that can exempt you from all governmental regulations.

The ultimate governmental interference from which none of us can escape is taxation. In a sole proprietorship the business is taxed the same as an individual.

As a sole proprietor who utilizes the services of others you pay employees wages, salaries, or commissions. You must pay rent to the landlord or bailor, and interest to whoever loans you money. If there are losses you must bear them alone. If there are profits you do not have to share them with a partner or stockholders.

In other words, as a sole proprietor you are the "boss." You personally employ others as employees or agents. The business contracts, those made by you personally or by your agents within their actual or apparent authority make you responsible for the obligations arising therefrom.

As in a partnership, you are responsible directly for torts or other legal liabilities incurred by you or by employees in the course and scope of authority. Your personal liability, therefore, is unlimited, subject to possible protection by contractual stipulation or insurance. To the extent that most of your personal assets might already be invested in the business, limited personal liability would not add much benefit as a practical matter. Credit can be had for the business to the extent of your business assets as well as your personal assets.

While there are no formalities or significant expenses involved in starting a business as a sole proprietor, there is always the need for capital for the operation of the business. As the sole owner you must rely entirely upon your own assets and credit for financing the business. Although there is little restriction on your doing business in other jurisdictions, such activity might make you amenable to process there.

If a fictitious name is used there are requirements in all states for registration of the trade name—or fictitious name. One may not, of course, use a name that would constitute unfair competition, confusion, trademark infringement, or invasion of right of privacy.

While the sole proprietor is not bothered by problems of management and control, or relations with co-owners, there is the potential for problems with employees or agents. You retain all the profits of the business and likewise must bear all the losses and you remain fully liable for any business debts when the business is dissolved.

There is generally no continuity of existence because on the death of the proprietor, the proprietorship obviously ends. However, some continuity may be obtained by a proper testamentary disposition. Thus, you may vest authority in your executor to continue the business so that your legatees may receive a going concern, thereby technically starting a new individual proprietorship. Actually, there are some better methods and techniques, beyond the scope of this work, for passing along a business to successors by the use of private annuities or living trusts. To the extent that the business did not depend upon the personal efforts of the sole owner, the business might thereafter be carried on by a new owner.

The interest of an individual proprietor in the business is freely transferable with a few possible exceptions. Marital rights, such as dower, curtesy, or other statutory elective rights, bulk transfer laws, and fraudulent conveyance laws may place some restrictions on the sale of the business. The bulk transfer laws prevents the defeat of the interests of business creditors by the sale of a going concern.

Your business income and other income, business losses and other losses, are treated together for tax purposes. Capital gains possibilities exist upon the sale of the business.

The dissolution or winding up of a sole proprietorship business is as simple and easy as it is to start.

Conclusion

The discussion of small business enterprises — corporations, partnerships and sole proprietorships — in three separate parts, and the analysis of the criteria for selection of a proper form of business organization for your business is not meant to suggest any competition among the entrants. Indeed, you may wish to use one, two, three or more of the forms of business entities discussed herein. It depends entirely upon your own business needs, and these needs may vary from time to time and from economic cycle to economic cycle.

Your selection of a form of business organization depends largely upon your own needs at any particular time, place, or circumstance. Your needs will be reflected by your business plans, and your selection of a form of business organization is not a means to an end, but merely a vehicle upon which you can achieve the planned results.

In fact, it frequently happens that a new business enterprise can start as a sole proprietorship, and when expansion generates a need for more capital, management and additional people, you may want to convert to a partnership or a corporation.

It is my hope that with the information discussed in this book you will be able to handle any aspect of your needs. You may need professional assistance from a lawyer or other advisers in some situations. This guide is designed to help you handle many of the so-called *legal* transactions yourself, with or without a lawyer, and to help you work efficiently and effectively with your professional advisers. Aside from the financial rewards of your business enterprises, your business success can give you and your associates a wealth of intangible benefits.

True success and happiness is a state of mind and must come to you through recognition of your own power and the finding of your own place in the world.

Appendix A
Statements of Corporate Purposes in Articles of Incorporation

General or Blanket Purpose Clauses

Sample 1: To manufacture, purchase, or otherwise acquire, own, mortgage, pledge, sell, assign, and transfer, or otherwise dispose of, to invest, trade, deal in and deal with, goods, wares and merchandise and real and personal property of every class and description.

Sample 2: To engage in any commercial, industrial, and agricultural enterprise calculated or designed to be profitable to this corporation and in conformity with the laws of the states in which business is transacted;

To generally engage in, do, and perform, any enterprises, act, or vocation that a natural person might or could do or perform;

To engage in the manufacture, sale, purchase, importing, and exporting of merchandise and personal property of all manner and description, to act as agents for the purchase, sale, and handling of goods, wares, and merchandise of any and all types and descriptions for the amount of the corporation or as factor, agent, procurer, or otherwise for or on behalf of another.

Sample 3: To manufacture, produce, purchase, or otherwise acquire, sell, or otherwise dispose of, import, export, distribute, deal in and with, whether as principal or agent, goods, wares, merchandise, and materials of every kind and description, whether now known or hereafter to be discovered or invented.

Sample 4: The purposes for which the corporation is formed are:

a. To engage primarily in the specific business of selling, buying, manufacturing, marketing, and distributing real and personal property of every kind and description.

b. To engage generally in the business of retail and wholesale selling, advertising, and marketing of services of every kind and description.

c. To engage in any business, related or unrelated to those described in clauses *a* and *b* of this Article, from time to time authorized or approved by the board of directors of this corporation or carry on any other trade or business which can, in the opinion of the board of directors of the company, be advantageously carried on in connection with or auxiliary to those described in clauses *a* and *b* of this Article, and to do all such things as are incidental or conducive to the attainment of the above objects or any of them.

d. To become a member of any partnership or joint venture and to enter into any lawful arrangement for sharing profits and/or losses in any transaction or transactions, and to promote and organize other corporations.

e. To do business anywhere in the world.

f. To have and to exercise all rights and powers that are now or may hereafter be granted to a corporation by law.

g. To have and to exercise all rights and powers that are now or may hereafter be granted to a corporation by law.

h. To acquire, hold, lease, encumber, convey, or otherwise dispose of real and personal property within or without the state, and take real and personal property by will, gift, or bequest.

i. To assume any obligations, enter into any contracts, or do any acts incidental to the transaction of its business or to the issue or sale of its securities, or expedient for the attainment of its obligations by mortgage or otherwise.

j. To borrow money and issue bonds, debentures, notes and evidences of indebtedness, and secure the payment of performance of its obligations by mortgage or otherwise.

k. To acquire, subscribe for, hold, own, pledge, and otherwise dispose of and represent shares of stock, bonds, and securities of any other corporation, domestic or foreign.

l. To purchase or otherwise acquire its own bonds, debentures, or other evidences of its indebtedness or obligation, and, subject to the provisions of the corporation laws of the state of incorporation, purchase or otherwise acquire its own shares.

m. Subject to the provisions of these Articles, to redeem shares thereby made subject to redemption.

n. To make donations for the public welfare or for charitable, scientific, or education purposes.

o. To sue and be sued in any court.

p. To adopt, use, and at will, alter a corporate seal, but failure to affix a seal shall not affect the validity of any instrument.

q. To make bylaws.

r. To appoint such subordinate officers or agents as its business may require, and to allow them suitable compensation.

The foregoing shall be construed as objects, purposes, and powers, and the enumeration thereof shall not be held to limit or restrict in any manner the powers now or hereafter conferred on this corporation by the laws of the state of incorporation or any state within which business may be carried on.

The objects, purposes, and powers specified herein shall, except as otherwise expressed, be in no way limited or restricted by reference to or inference from the terms of any purposes, and powers specified in each of the clauses or paragraphs of these Articles of Incorporation shall be regarded as independent objects, purposes, or powers.

The corporation may in its bylaws confer powers, not in conflict with law, upon its directors in addition to the foregoing and in addition to the powers and authorities expressly conferred upon them by statute.

Additional Clauses for Specific Businesses

Agency and Business Promotion

To transact the business of advertising, promoting, and developing the business of other corporations, partnerships, or individuals for hire, or upon commission, or otherwise, by and through the means of preparing advertising for other corporations, partnerships, or individuals, and of advertising the business, commodities, or other property, real, personal, or mixed, of other corporations, partnerships, or individuals in newspapers, books, booklets, prospectuses, magazines, circulars, pamphlets, or other similar literature and advertising media.

Art and Artists' Supplies Dealer

To carry on the business of holders of exhibitions and dealers in pictures, and makers and sellers of picture frames, artists' colors, oils, paints, paint brushes, and other instruments, articles, and ingredients relating to any such business.

Bookstore

To conduct and carry on in all of its branches and business of buying, selling, and dealing in and with books of any and all kinds, whether new or old, and manuscripts, prints, engravings, lithographs, pamphlets, writings, publications, stationery, and similar goods or merchandise; to conduct the business of an agency in all of its branches for any and all of the goods or merchandise; to acquire and carry on a selling agency or agencies for the sale of any and all merchandise pertaining or relating to books, manuscripts, prints, engravings, lithographs, pamphlets, writings, and similar goods or merchandise; to deal in and with goods, wares, and merchandise and personal property of every and any sort, nature, or description.

Farm Ownership and Farming

To purchase, own, improve, equip, operate, and manage farms and engage in any agricultural pursuit or undertaking.

Groceries

To merchandise, sell, offer for sale, and distribute at wholesale and retail, foods and foodstuffs of all kinds and descriptions, whether in bulk, package, bottle, or can, including beverages of all kinds and for all purposes, and to generally deal in groceries and grocery products suitable for public consumption.

Hardware Store

To engage in and operate a general hardware and mercantile business and to deal in, buy, and sell general hardware, electrical and gas appliances, housewares, toys, general merchandise including paints and painting supplies, but not excluding any other articles of merchandise sometimes dealt in by hardware establishments.

Marketing

To enter into contracts or agreements relating to sales campaigns and marketing and to the design, manufacture, operation, and use of tools and tooling of every kind, character, and description, including, without being limited to, mechanical, pneumatic, hydraulic, electrical, or artistic devices, articles, or designs with any and all persons, firms, corporations, or other legal entity, whether domestic or foreign.

Retail Stores

To establish, purchase, lease, as lessee, or otherwise acquire, to own, operate, and maintain, and to sell mortgage, lease or lessor, and otherwise dispose of retail stores or departments therein and to conduct a general merchandising business therein.

Appendix B
Names and Addresses of State Offices Where New Corporation Papers Are Filed

Secretary of State
Corporations Division
524 State Office Building
Montgomery, AL 36130

Department of Commerce
  and Economic
  Development
Corporations
Pouch D
Juneau, Alaska 99811

Arizona Corporation
  Commission
2222 West Encanto Blvd.
Phoenix, AZ 85009

Secretary of State
State Capitol
Little Rock, AR 72201

Secretary of State
111 Capitol Mall
Sacramento, CA 95814

Secretary of State
1575 Sherman Street
2nd Floor
Denver, CO 80203

Secretary of State
30 Trinity Street
Hartford, CT 06106

Department of State
Division of Corporations
Townsend Building
P.O. Box 898
Dover, DE 19901

Office of Superintendent of
  Corporations
Washington, D.C. 20000

Secretary of State
Capitol Building
Tallahassee, FL 32301

Secretary of State
Corporations Department
225 Peachtree St. N.E.
Atlanta, GA 30303

Department of Regulatory
Agencies
1010 Richards Street
Honolulu, HI 96813

Secretary of State
State of Idaho
Boise, ID 83720

Secretary of State
Springfield, IL 62756

Secretary of State
State House #155
Indianapolis, IN 46204

Secretary of State
State Capitol
Des Moines, IA 50319

Secretary of State
Capitol—2nd Floor
Topeka, KS 66612

Secretary of State
Capitol Building #150
Frankfort, KY 40601

Secretary of State
P.O. Box 44125
Baton Rouge, LA 70804

Secretary of State
State House Station 101
Augusta, ME 04333

State Department of
Assessments and Taxation
301 West Preston Street
Baltimore, MD 21201

Secretary of State
State House
Boston, MA 02133

Department of Commerce
Corporation Division
P.O. Box 30054
Lansing, MI 48909

Secretary of State
Corporation Division
180 State Office Building
St. Paul, MN 55155

Secretary of State
401 Mississippi Street
P.O. Box 136
Jackson, MS 39205

Secretary of State
State Capitol
Helena, MT 59620

Department of State
Lincoln, NE 68509

Secretary of State
Carson City, NV 89710

Secretary of State
State House
Concord, NH 03301

Department of State
Trenton, NJ 08625

State Corporation
Commission
P.O. Box 1269
Sante Fe, NM 87501

Department of State
162 Washington Ave.
Albany, NY 12231

Secretary of State
116 West Jones Street
Raleigh, NC 27603

Secretary of State
Bismarck, ND 58505

Secretary of State
30 East Broad Street
14th Floor
Columbus, OH 43215

Secretary of State
101 State Capitol
Oklahoma City, OK 73105

Department of Commerce
Corporation Division
Commerce Building
Salem, OR 97310

Department of State
Room 308
North Office Building
Harrisburg, PA 17120

Secretary of State
Providence, RI 02903

Secretary of State
P.O. Box 11350
Columbia, SC 29211

Secretary of State
State Capitol Building
Pierre, SD 57501

Department of State
Fifth Floor
Nashville, TN 37219

Secretary of State
Corporations Division
Austin, TX 78711

Secretary of State
Salt Lake City, UT 84100

Secretary of State
Pavilion Office Building
Montpelier, VT 05601

State Corporation
Commission
Box 1197
Richmond, VA 23209

Secretary of State
Olympia, WA 98501

Secretary of State
Charleston, WV 25305

Secretary of State
Corporations Division
Box 7846
Madison, WI 53707

Secretary of State
State Capitol
Cheyenne, WY 82002

Glossary of Legal Terms

Accommodation: An arrangement or engagement made as a favor to another, not upon a consideration received; something done to oblige, usually a loan of money or commercial paper; a friendly agreement or composition of differences.

Accommodation Note: One to which the accommodating party has put his name, without consideration, to accommodate some other party, who is to issue it and is expected to pay it.

Accommodation Party: One who has signed an instrument as maker, drawer, acceptor, or endorser without receiving value for it and for the purpose of lending his name to some other person as means of securing credit.

Acknowledgment: An acknowledgment is a public declaration or formal statement of a person executing an instrument made to the official authorized to take the acknowledgment, that the execution of the first instrument was his free act and deed. The written evidence of an acknowledgment, which states in substance that the person named herein was known to and appeared before him and acknowledged the instrument to be his act and deed. Generally substantial compliance with the form or requirements laid down in the state statute is essential to the validity of a certificate of acknowledgment. An acknowledgment to an instrument generally has three functions: it may give validity to the instrument; it may permit the instrument to be introduced in evidence without proof of execution; or it may entitle the instrument to be recorded.

Action: A suit or process at law; the procedure of instituting a law suit in a court of law.

Affidavit: A written declaration under oath; a statement of facts in writing signed by the party, and sworn to or confirmed by declaration before an authorized magistrate or notary public.

Agent: An agent is one who, by the authority of a principal undertakes to transact some business or manage some affairs on account of the principal, and to render an account of it. He is a substitute, or deputy, appointed by his principal primarily to bring about business relations between the principal and third persons.

Ambiguous: Doubtfulness, doubleness of meaning; duplicity; indistinctness, or uncertainty of meaning of an expression used in written instrument. A want of clearness or definiteness; difficult to comprehend or distinguish; likely to be interpreted two ways; equivocal; indefinite.

Anticipatory Breach: In contract, a breach prior to a duty to perform, indicating an intention not to perform.

Arbitrary: Given, adjudged, or done according to one's will or discretion; decided by an arbiter rather than by law; capricious; despotic; imperious; tyrannical; uncontrolled.

Arbitration: The act of arbitrating; the hearing and determination of a cause between parties in controversy, by a person or persons chosen by the parties.

Articles of Incorporation: An instrument by which a private corporation is formed and organized under the general corporation laws.

Articles of Partnership: A written agreement by which the parties enter into a co-partnership upon the terms and conditions stipulated in the contract.

Assignment: An assignment is a contract. It is a transfer or setting over of some right or interest in property, or of property itself, from one person to another.

Assignment for the Benefit of Creditors: The transfer by a debtor, without consideration, of part or all of his property to a party in trust to apply it to the payment of the debtor's indebtedness, with the surplus, if any, being returned to the debtor. It vests legal title in the assignee as trustee and places the property beyond the control of the assignor or the reach of his creditors, except as they have a right under the assignment to share in his estate.

Authorize: To give authority, warrant, or legal power to; to give a right to act; to empower; to make legal; to establish by authority or by usage or public opinion; to warrant; to sanction; to justify.

Bad Faith: The opposite of *good faith,* generally implying or involving actual or constructive fraud, or a design to mislead or deceive another, or a neglect or refusal to fulfill some duty or some contractual obligation, not promoted by an honest mistake or to one's rights or duties, but by some interest or sinister motive.

Bankrupt: Originally and strictly, a trader who secrets himself or does certain other acts tending to defraud his creditors. A person who has committed an act of bankruptcy; one who has done some act or suffered some act to be done in consequences of which, under the laws of his country, he is liable to be proceeded against by his creditors for the seizure and distribution among them of his entire property.

Blue Sky Laws: A popular name for acts providing for the regulation and supervision of investment companies, for the protection of the community from investing in fraudulent companies. A law intended to stop the sale of stock in fly-by-night concerns, visionary oil wells, distant gold mines, and other similar fraudulent exploitations.

Board of Directors: The governing body of a private corporation.

Bond: In law, any written and sealed obligation, especially one requiring payment of a stipulated amount of money on or before a given date. A sum of money paid as bail or surety. One who acts as bail; bondsman.

Book Value of Stock: The net worth as shown by the books of the company; the net worth of all corporate assets less all liabilities, without allowing for the item of good will, unless it is shown clearly to be of certain value.

Breach of Contract: Failure, without legal excuse, to perform any promise which forms the whole or part of a contract.

Bylaws: A rule or law of a corporation for its government which prescribes the rights and duties of the members with reference to the internal government of the corporation, the management of its affairs, and the rights and duties existing between the members.

Capital: That portion of the assets of a corporation, regardless of their source, which is utilized for the conduct of the corporate business and for the purpose of deriving gains and profits.

Capital Stock: The amount of money, property, or other means authorized by its charter and contributed, or agreed to be contributed, by the shareholders as the financial basis for the pursuit of the business of the corporation, such contribution being made either directly through stock subscription or indirectly through the declaration of stock dividends.

Cash Dividend: The distribution to shareholders of a portion of the profits or surplus assets of a corporation.

Close Corporation: A corporation in which the majority of the stock is held by the officers and directors. For example, a corporation owned and operated primarily by a single family.

Commerce: The exchange of goods, productions, or property of any kind. Intercourse by way of trade and traffic between different peoples or states and the citizens or inhabitants thereof, including not only the purchase, sale, and exchange of commodities, but also the instrumentalities and agencies by which it is promoted and the means and activities by which it is carried on, and the transportation of persons as well as of goods, both by land and by sea.

Internal commerce is that which is carried on between individuals within the same state, or between different parts of the same state.

Interstate commerce is that between states or nations entirely foreign to each other.

Intrastate commerce is that which is begun, carried on, and completed wholly within the limits of a single state, as contrasted with "interstate" commerce.

Commercial Paper: Bills of exchange, promissory notes, bank checks, and other negotiable instruments for the payment of money. Commercial paper is used to facilitate business transactions, as a substitute for the payment of money directly, and affords to the debtor an extension of time for the actual payment while offering certain protections and safeguards to all parties involved.

Common Law: The general and ordinary law of a community receiving its binding force from universal reception. Historically, that body of law and juristic theory which was originated, developed, and formulated in England.

Consign: To deliver goods to a carrier to be transmitted to a designated factor or agent. To deliver or transfer as a charge or trust; to commit, in trust, give in trust, to transfer from oneself to the care of another; to send or transmit goods to a merchant, factor, or agent for sale; to deposit with another to be sold, disposed of, or called for.

Consignment: The act or process of consigning goods; the consigning of goods or cargo, especially to an agent for sale or custody; goods sent to a retailer who is expected to pay following sale.

Continuity: The state or quality of being continuous; a continuous or connected whole.

Contract: A promise, or set of promises, for the breach of which the law gives a remedy, or for the performance of which the law in some way recognizes a duty.

Corporation: An artificial person or legal entity created by or under the authority of the laws of a state or nation, composed, in some instances, of a single person and his successors, or another corporation, being the incumbents of a particular office, but ordinarily consisting of an association of individuals, who subsist as a body politic under a special denomination, which is regarded in law as having a personality and existence distinct from that of its members, and which is, by the same authority, vested with the capacity of continuous succession, irrespective of changes in the membership, either in perpetuity or for a limited term of years, and of acting as a unit or single individual in matters relating to the common purpose of the association, within the scope of the powers and authorities conferred upon such bodies by law.

Doing Business: Within statutes on service of process on foreign corporations, equivalent to conducting or managing business. A foreign corporation is *doing business*, making it amenable to process within a state, if it does business in the state in such a manner as to warrant the inference that it is present there—or that it has subjected itself to the jurisdiction and laws in which the service is made. The doing of business is the exercise in the state of some of the ordinary functions for which the corporation was organized. What constitutes doing business depends on the facts in each particular case.

Domestic Corporation: A corporation incorporated under the laws of a state, as opposed to a foreign corporation under the laws of another state or nation.

Dormant Partner: A partner whose name is not used by the firm, and who is generally unknown to those dealing with the partnership.

Entity: A real being, existence.

Equitable: Possessing or exhibiting equity; equal in regard to the rights of persons; just; fair; impartial; pertaining to a court of equity.

Equitable Estoppel: That condition in which justice forbids one to gainsay his own acts or assertions. The preclusion of person by his act or conduct or silence from asserting rights which might otherwise have existed. The species of estoppel which equity put upon a person who has made a false representation or a concealment of material facts, with knowledge of the facts, to a party ignorant of the truth of the matter, with the intention that the other party should act upon it, and with the result that such party is actually induced to act upon it, to his damage.

Elements or essentials of such estoppel include change of position for the worse by party asserting estoppel.

Such estoppel may be based on acts, omissions to act, representations, admissions, concealment or silence.

False Representation: A representation which is untrue, willfully made to deceive another to his injury.

Fiduciary: The term is derived from the Roman law, and, as a noun, means a person holding the character of a trustee, or the trust and confidence involved in it and the scrupulous good faith and candor which it requires. A person having a duty to act primarily for the benefit of another in matters connected with the undertaking. As an adjective it means something in the nature of a trust, having the characteristics of a trust, analogous to a trust, relating to or founded upon a trust or confidence.

Foreign Corporation: A corporation created by or under the authority of the laws of another state, government, or country.

Fraud: An intentional perversion of truth for the purpose of inducing another, in reliance upon it, to part with some valuable thing belonging to him or to surrender a legal right; a false representation of a matter of fact, whether by words or by conduct, by false or misleading representations, or by concealment of that which should have been disclosed, which deceives, and is intended to deceive another so that he shall act upon it to his legal detriment.

Indemnity: A collateral contract or assurance, by which one person engages to secure another against an anticipated loss or to prevent him from being damaged by the legal consequences of an act or forebearance on the part of the parties or of some third person.

Independent Contractor: One who, in exercising an independent employment, contracts to do certain work according to his own methods, without being subject to the control of his employer, except as to the product or result of his work. The basic element of an independent contractor relationship is the fact that the contractor has an independent business or occupation. In general, it excludes the relation of principal and agent, master and servant, and the traditional employer-employee status.

Indicia: Signs; indications; circumstances which point to the existence of a given fact as probable, but not certain. For example, indicia of partnership are any circumstances which would induce the belief that a given person was in reality, though not ostensibly, a member of a given firm.

Insolvency: The condition of a person who is insolvent, an inability to pay one's debts, having a lack of means to pay one's debts. One who is unable to pay debts as they fall due, or in the usual course of trade or business.

Joint Tenancy: Common ownership of property by two or more persons, with the property passing on to the surviving person or persons in case of the death of one co-owner.

Joint Venture: An association of two or more persons to carry out a single business for profit which is usually, but not necessarily, limited to a single transaction.

Law Merchant: An expression substantially equivalent to the mercantile law or commercial law. It designates the system of rules, customs, and usages generally recognized and adopted by merchants and traders, and which, either in its simplicity or as modified by common law or statutes, constitutes the law for the regulation of their transactions and the solution of their controversies.

Liable: Answerable for consequences; under obligation legally to make good a loss; responsible; apt or likely to incur something undesirable; susceptible; subject or exposed to.

Limited Partnership: A partnership in which the liability of some members, but not all, is limited; such a partnership may be formed under most state statutes, which permit an individual to contribute a specific sum of money to the capital of the partnership and limit his liability for losses to that amount, upon the partnership complying with the requirements of the statute.

Litigation: The act or process of litigating; the proceedings in a suit at law; a lawsuit.

Long Arm Statute: A statute allowing a court to obtain jurisdiction over a defendant located outside the normal jurisdiction of the court.

Majority Shareholders: Holders of more than 50 percent of the stock of a corporation.

Minority Shareholders: Holders of less than 50 percent of the stock of a corporation.

Minutes: Memoranda or notes of a transaction or proceeding. Thus, the record of the proceedings at a meeting of directors of corporations or shareholders is called *minutes.*

Misrepresentation: Any manifestation by words or other conduct by one person to another that, under the circumstances, amounts to an assertion not in accordance with the facts. An untrue statement of fact. An incorrect or false representation. That which, if accepted, leads the mind to an apprehension of a condition other and different from that which exists. False and fraudulent misrepresentation is a representation contrary to the fact, made by a person with a knowledge of its falsehood, and being the cause of the other party's entering into the contract. Negligent misrepresentation is a false representation made by a person who has no reasonable grounds for believing it to be true, though he does not know that it is untrue, or even believes it to be true.

Monopolies, Restraints of Trade, and Unfair Trade Practices: During the latter part of the nineteenth century this country had great growth in its economic and industrial development. There was a vast accumulation of wealth in the hands of corporations and individuals, and an enormous development of corporate organizations with the facility for combining into "trusts." As a result competition was threatened, price control was feared, and individual initiative was dampened—the evils that flow from monopoly practices.

In July 1890, Congress passed the *Sherman Antitrust Act,* 15 U.S.C. 1-7, which declared illegal all contracts, combinations, or conspiracies in restraint of trade or commerce among the states or territories or with foreign nations, and outlawed combinations or conspiracies to monopolize interstate or foreign trade or commerce.

The *Clayton Act,* 15 U.S.C. 18, was enacted in 1914 to reach certain specified practices which had been held by the courts to be outside the ambit of the Sherman Act. The purpose was to prevent economic concentration in American economy by keeping a large number of small competitors in business.

The *Robinson-Patman Act,* 15 U.S.C. 13, enacted in 1936, had as its main purpose to strengthen the Clayton Act regarding price discrimination.

Many of the states also have enacted antitrust laws; they are sometimes called "little Sherman Acts."

No Par Stock: Stock which is issued by a corporation without nominal value.

Par Value: The amount shown due on the face of the stock certificate.

Partnership: A voluntary contract between two or more competent persons to place their money, effects, labor, and skill, or some of them, in lawful commerce or business, with the understanding that there shall be proportional sharing of the profits and losses between them. An association of two or more persons to carry on as co-owners a business for profit.

Perpetual: Never ceasing; continuous; enduring; lasting; unlimited in respect of time; continuing without intermission or interval.

Piercing the Corporate Veil: In cases involving fraud or unjust enrichment, where the court refuses to recognize a corporation as an entity separate from those responsible for corporate activity, holding the corporation's alter ego liable, the court is said to pierce the corporate veil.

Profits: Any advantage, benefit, or return; pecuniary gain; the advantage or gain resulting to the owner of capital from its employment in any undertaking; the excess of income over expenditure, specifically the difference, when an excess, between the original cost and selling price of anything; the ratio in any year of this gain to the sum invested; revenue from investments or property.

Qualification: The process by which a foreign corporation signifies its presence in the state and by which it submits itself to the laws and conditions of admission to do business in the state as prescribed by the laws.

Quorum: A majority of the entire body; such a number of the members of a body as is competent to transact business in the absence of the other members. The idea of a quorum is that, when that required number of persons goes into a session as a body, such as directors of a corporation, the votes of a majority thereof are sufficient for binding action.

Sale: A contract between a seller and a buyer, or purchaser, by which the seller, in consideration of the payment or promise of payment of a certain price in money, transfers to the purchaser the title and the possession of property.

Service of Process: The service of writs, summonses, rules, and other documents signifies the delivering to or leaving them with the party to whom or with whom they ought to be delivered or left; and, when they are so delivered, they are then said to have been served. Usually a copy only is served and the original is shown. Substituted service of process is accomplished by mailing a copy to the defendant and, in some instances publishing notice in a newspaper.

Share of Stock: The right which an owner has in the management, profits and ultimate assets of the corporation.

Shareholder: A person owning some part of the stock of a corporation.

Silent Partner: A partner whose connection with the partnership business is concealed and does not generally take any active part in the business.

Statute: An enactment of the legislative body of a government that is formally expressed and documented as a law; written, as opposed to common law. A permanent rule or law enacted by the governing body of a corporation or institution.

Statute of Limitations: A statute imposing limits on the period during which certain rights, as the collection of debts, may be legally enforced.

Summons: A writ, directed to the sheriff or other proper officer, requiring him to notify the person named that an action has been commenced against him in the court whence the writ issues, and that he is required to appear, on a day named, and answer the complaint in such action.

Trade Name: A name used in trade to designate a particular business of certain individuals considered somewhat as an entity, or the place at which a business is located, or of a class of goods, but which is not a technical trade mark either because not applied or affixed to goods sent into the market or because not capable of exclusive appropriation by anyone as a trademark. Trade names may, or may not, be exclusive.

Trustee: One to whom property or funds have been legally entrusted to be administered for the benefit of another; a person, usually one of a body of persons, appointed to administer the affairs of a company, institution, or the like.

Usury: An illegal contract for a loan or forbearance of money, goods, or things in action, by which illegal interest is reserved, or agreed to be reserved or taken. An unconscionable and exorbitant rate or amount of interest.

Winding Up: The administration of assets for the purpose of terminating the business and discharging the obligations of the partnership to its members.

Writ of Attachment: A writ employed to enforce obedience to an order or judgment of the court. It may take the form of commanding the sheriff to attach the disobedient party and to have him before the court to answer his contempt.

Index